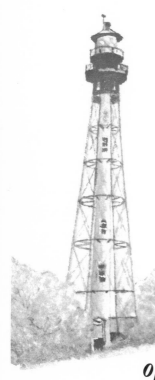

Cap'n Charlie
and Lights
of the Lower Cape Fear

ETHEL HERRING

To

"The Professor"

my husband-Owen

CONTENTS

Charles Norton Swan 1873-1964

CAP'N CHARLIE
AND
LIGHTS OF THE
LOWER CAPE FEAR

Keeper of the Lights! Cap'n Charlie wore this title as a king wears his crown or a soldier his medals. He had an humble pride in his work. To him, this title carried with it honor, responsibility, and sacrifice.

Captain Charles Norton Swan crowded into his ninety-one years an unbelievable amount of adventure, experience, and service. His entire life was spent on, in, or near the sea. For him to have moved inland, would have been like taking a lively bluefish out of water.

He began his life's voyage August 19, 1873, at Amelia Lighthouse, near Fernandina, Florida, and it ended quietly in his sleep at his home port of Southport, North Carolina, September 27, 1964. For nearly a century Cap'n Charlie lived one of the most exciting and interesting lives in our state's history.

This was a quiet man, short of stature, immaculate in his dress. His eyes were like part of the deep sea he loved so dearly. His ruddy skin let those who met him know he had lived out in the sun from his early youth. As he grew older his hair became iron gray. Cap'n Charlie wore crisp khaki for everyday, but, of course, he wore his dark blue serge dress uniform to church and public meetings. He always looked as if he had just brushed up for inspection. However, there was usually a jaunty little tilt to his white top officer's cap.

Truly, Cap'n Charlie Swan made his X mark on the map and in the hearts of all those who knew him.

As many times a doctor's son becomes interested in medicine, a circus man's son in the circus and so on — it is perhaps even more true with the men of the sea. Theirs is an entirely different world. Their language is distinctive. Their family stories are not of deep snows in the mountains or of camping by a lake. Their knowledge of the unpredictable ways of the sea is valuable and learned through experience.

It is not strange that in the Swan family alone there have been light keepers, river pilots, and seafaring men for five generations. To many members of these families there is no finer way to work than on board a ship. They say, "It's in the blood". Could be, but if this is true, the "sea in the blood" doesn't thin their courage, strength, and integrity.

To know a man like Cap'n Charlie is one thing, but to know what makes him that kind of man is quite another.

There can be no doubt about the lasting influence Cap'n Charlie's father had on his son's life. Through the years of his boyhood he was very close to his father. He heard tales of the years of the War between the States, of the blockade runners and their daring. He knew courage at first hand and some of it rubbed off on him.

Perhaps as we learn something of his father's life we can see many definite examples of his influence on young Charlie.

CAPTAIN HANS SVANG

Captain Hans Svang (meaning "owner of land") was born December 10, 1830, in Kragero, near Bergen, Norway. Sometime during his early life he changed his name to Henry Greenwood Swan. This young Norwegian went to sea at the age of sixteen on a barkentine, a three-masted vessel. He sailed around the world and learned much about the ways of the sea.

When Henry Swan was in New York he met, fell in love with, and, in due time, married a Swedish girl. His young wife went on the sailing vessels with her husband. Their first two sons, George and Fred, were born at sea. George became associated with the river and harbor pilots of Charleston, South Carolina, and was at one time president of the Pilot's Association. Fred became an executive with the Erie Railroad in New York. A third son, Louis, was drowned at seventeen, off a pilot boat on which he was an apprentice. Captain Henry's first wife died of yellow fever in Georgetown, South Carolina.

During the War Between the States, Captain Henry was a courageous blockade runner. These ships exchanged cotton and tobacco from Wilmington for Nassau's foodstuffs such as sugar, coffee and molasses, as well as clothing, blankets, and munitions from England and other countries.

In an official record (vol. 9 p 519 Report of John J. Almy, Commander of the *USS Connecticut* — March 1, 1864) we read:

"I have the pleasure to inform you that this morning at nine o'clock the English blockade runner *Scotia*, Henry Swan, Master, was captured by this steamer, after a chase of two hours. This capture was 85 miles SSE of Cape Fear. The Captain admits that he left Wilmington last night with 220 bales of cotton on board. The *Scotia* is a side-wheel, iron steamer built at Glasgow and this was his third trip to Wilmington".

An official record of February 17, 1864 tells of the bringing in of supplies — blankets, shoes, and provisions — aboard the

Spunkie, another blockade runner mastered by Captain Henry. This steamer was run ashore by the Yankees near Fort Caswell, while trying to get in. The cargo was removed (perhaps to Fort Caswell), but the vessel "was a wreck, having been broken in two".

Captain Henry was master of several ships. Once he was captured and placed in a hotel on Meeting Street in Charleston which at the time was being used as a temporary prison. He was rationed out the usual amount of whiskey. Captain Henry gave his to the guards. When they were drunk enough not to notice him, he dropped out a second story window. This was his only possible way of escape. His suspenders caught on the iron hooks of the window shutters on the first story. He finally managed to tear himself loose and fall to the ground, but in doing so Captain Henry broke his ankle. A less determined man would have given up, but his life was at stake.

In the dark of the night the Captain crawled past King Street. This was a slow and painful experience. Just before dawn a negro man with a horse and cart came by. Captain Henry asked if he would carry him to the north of town where he had Norwegian friends.

"No, sir, Yankees would kill me!"

"How about a hundred-dollar bill?"

"I never saw one before. Let's go."

So the negro man put Captain Henry in the back of his cart and covered him with straw. They began the slow, dangerous journey across town to the settlement of Norwegian friends.

It must have been a sight to see when Captain Henry Swan (Hans Svang) crawled out from a load of straw, with a broken ankle, heavy beard, and a hungry body. His friends took him in and protected him until he was able to get out and go back to run the blockade in his beloved ships.

Getting back to the ships was not a simple thing to do, especially in time of war. There was danger and much difficulty involved. He made his way to the docks and got aboard a ship as a deck hand. He had grown a heavy beard as a disguise so the enemy would not recognize him as the captain who had been their prisoner. Captain Henry gave the ship's master one thousand dollars to go off his course to take him to his wife in Nassau. Later he worked his way back to Charleston and became Master of another blockade runner, the *Florence*.

When Captain Henry was carrying cotton out for Sprunt Cotton Company the pay was in silver and gold. There were no safes as now, so money aboard ships was carried in sealed oak kegs of different sizes. Captain Henry had orders from the cotton company to throw the kegs overboard if captured to keep the money from the enemy. This the Captain had to do off Fort Fisher. He was being chased so closely that he had to make the difficult decision to obey the orders or risk the enemy's capturing the gold. Almost immediately a heavy fog set in and Captain Henry was able to outrun his pursuers. This experience seemed to bother him as long as he lived.

Near the end of the War, Captain Henry was taken prisoner at Corncake Inlet. He usually brought his ship in under the cover of darkness through Corncake. The Captain did not know of the fall of Fort Fisher. In the darkness just before daylight he heard the splash of oars in the water and thought this was a Confederate boat. Instead, it was the Yankees. They boarded the *Florence* and took the Captain and the entire crew prisoners. After Captain Henry had been in prison eight days, it was learned that he was not an American citizen; therefore the Federal forces could not hold him. They did hold several members of the crew, however.

On his countless trips to Nassau, Captain Swan had met a beautiful, young English woman, Caroline Ann Smith. Her father owned a large plantation in the Bahamas. In 1863 the Captain and lovely Caroline were married in Nassau.

At the close of hostilities Captain Henry was near Smithville, North Carolina (now Southport). He had become strongly attached to this part of the world and decided to settle down. He was about thirty-five years of age.

Amelia Island Lighthouse

Captain Swan entered the Lighthouse Service. He and his family lived in Georgetown, South Carolina, until 1873, when he was transferred to Fernandina, Florida, to be tender of the Amelia Island Lighthouse. Fernandina Beach is just south of the Georgia state line, near the mouth of the St. Mary's River. The masonry tower was built in 1839, with a spiral stairway of granite.

Here, on August 19, 1873, the Swan's fifth child was born — Charles Omega Swan. Later, after the birth of a sixth child, his name was changed to Charles Norton Swan.

CHARLIE'S BOYHOOD

The family was transferred to Cumberland Island, Georgia, in 1877. This island was, in many ways, similar to Bald Head Island (Smith Island) at the mouth of North Carolina's Cape Fear River, therefore very familiar to Captain Henry from blockade days.

Playing in the yard near a pot in which a ham was cooking, four year old Charlie accidentally burned his right hand so badly that the two small fingers were always bent.

Happy days were spent on the island when young Charlie and his brother Gus, three years older, played in the creeks. They learned to protect themselves from dangers of the water. Charlie learned to use a heavy gun when he was eight or nine. He could swim like a fish. He and Gus would scare the alligators out to the other little creeks, then dive in for their fun.

One day the boys were squirrel hunting. Mr. O'Hagan's young calf looked like a deer through the brush, so Gus shot the calf. When they saw what had happened they ran to their father. Charlie said, "Gus did it, I didn't — Gus did it, I didn't!" Both boys got good lickings, Charlie for telling on Gus and Gus for shooting the calf. Captain Henry had to pay dearly for Mr. O'Hagan's loss.

Once when Charlie was about ten, he was cleaning his gun. It accidentally went off, barely missing one of his sisters. This taught him a lesson he never forgot. He remembered it years later when he had children of his own. He and their Uncle Gus taught Charlie's children to handle a gun, to shoot well, and to cast a net at an early age.

When he was eleven, Charlie's family moved to Southport. They lived in a big house on the corner of Davis and Moore Streets. This was the year young Charlie had yellow jaundice. He had to be in bed for one long year, a hard assignment for any boy. For one who had lived such an active life out in the open, it was like caging a gull. Somehow the twelve months finally passed and slowly Charlie regained his strength.

For many reasons he was able to go to school only about nine months in his life. He went to Mr. Sam Tharp for five months and to the old Academy for four months.

Charlie's mother died when he was young. The six sisters kept house for the father of this large family and the boys. Shortly after the mother's death Gus went to live with his half-brother Fred in New York. This left Charlie "the man of the house". Captain Henry was at this time Captain of the Frying Pan Lightship and of course was away from home a great deal of the time. The Lightship was anchored at the end of the dangerous Frying Pan Shoals, the narrow finger of rocky humps of land that extend 20-30 miles southeast from Cape Fear, the southern tip of Bald Head Island.

Young Charlie had a close friend, Ernest Burriss, who had his own skiff and nets. The boys grew up together almost as brothers. They sold oysters, clams, and fish to the boarding houses, and Charlie went from door to door with fish on a string to sell.

When he was fifteen he spent much time on the Lightship with his father. Years later he enjoyed telling the story of the time Captain Henry asked the Swedish steward aboard the Lightship to make a fruit duff for dessert. Came time for dinner and no duff. The Captain asked for an explanation. The steward answered in his broken English. "Cap'n, I've looked in all my cook books and I can't find it. If r-o-u-g-h spells rough, why don't d-o-u-g-h spell duff?" This was always funny to Charlie. He thought maybe the steward should have been right.

As the days came and went Charlie learned more and more about living on the briny deep and about courageous men. He did not know that soon his own courage was to be given a real test.

Late one afternoon on the Lightship, he was helping the Quartermaster raise the lantern to light for the night. The rope slipped out of his hand and the lantern fell, striking him on the right cheek. The blow knocked Charlie's right eye out of the socket.

Here they were, many miles from a doctor and no means of transportation. Something had to be done at once. First aid is required on all ships and government stations; a little manual of instructions and a small medicine chest were always aboard. Captain Henry made a pad of gauze, saturated in kerosene, and taped it over the eye, which was still out of socket.

Eight days passed before a pilot boat came near enough to the Lightship for the injured boy to get help. Charlie was sent in to Southport and taken to Dr. Watson at the Drug Store. The doctor replaced the eye and no trouble came from the accident. Charlie's eye lids were split, but no stitches were taken. There were always thin scars on the lids.

Another experience which tested Charlie's courage came when he was swimming alone and was attacked by a shark. As Charlie turned in the water he realized he was in trouble. The shark came up under his right side with his mouth open. The surprised swimmer kicked and frightened the shark away and headed for shore, not realizing the shark's teeth had ripped a six inch gash in his side until he was out of the water. Charlie carried this scar as long as he lived, a constant reminder of an ever present danger when in the water.

As a boy Charlie spent several months in the summer on Bald Head Island with Captain John L. Watts who was captain of the Life Saving Station (now Coast Guard). Mrs. Watts had been Miss Esther Dosher and everyone called her "Miss Ess". For thirty years her brother, Captain Sonny Dosher, was Keeper of the Bald Head Light Station. Each summer Captain Watts let the crew "take off" two months. Charlie was of real help to Captain Watts and "Miss Ess" while the men were away.

During these days young Charlie came to love Bald Head Island with an undying affection. Years later, when he entered the Lighthouse Service, his highest ambition was to return to Bald Head.

Here he learned to make the famous Turtle Egg Duff, a delicious desert. This is the receipe Cap'n Charlie gave to his daughter-in-law, Delores:

TURTLE EGG DUFF

INGREDIENTS:
2 dozen turtle egg yolks
½ cup granulated sugar
¾ cups self-rising flour
½ teaspoon salt
1 tablespoon shortening, melted
1 teaspoon vanilla extract
½ box of seedless raisins

DIRECTIONS:
Small amount of water
Whip yolks with fork until fluffy.
Add sugar to egg mixture
and blend well.
Sift flour and add with
salt & soda to above mixture.
Blend together well.
Add shortening and extract to above.
Dredge raisins in flour to
separate and keep from
sticking together and then
add to mixture.
Add a small amount of water
to above mixture. Just
enough to mix well. Pour
into a well greased duff mold.

First put on a large pot of water as this has to be boiling when the mold is put in to cook. The mold is bucket-shaped with a tube which allows the water to go up into mold to cook center done. It has a lid that clamps on. This mold is often called plum pudding or steam pudding mold. The mold is thoroughly greased including the inside lid before filling with above mixture. After mixture is added clamp the lid on tightly. If the pot of water is now boiling you are ready to put the mold in the pot. The water should reach about ¾ ways from the top of the mold. Cook standing up for approximately 45 minutes and then turn the mold upside down and cook for approximately 15-20 minutes longer. Remove mold from pot, removing lid turn mold upside down in a plate. The duff will be light golden brown. To test for doneness insert a case knife or some narrow sharp knife in the duff; it should come out clean. If the knife comes out sticky you can return to mold and pot and recook a few minutes longer. This duff is best when served immediately. It can be sliced any way desired. Serve topped with butter/sugar sauce. You can use any type sauce you desire. Serves 10-12.

CHARLIE GOES TO SEA

When Charlie was seventeen he went to sea in a three masted schooner, a brig named the *Water Witch*. He made many trips as a seaman from Boston to the islands in the Caribbean, following in his father's footsteps.

The King of one of the islands met their large sailing vessel on a trip. He was dressed in a snow white uniform, with much gold braid and trimming. This impressed Charlie, as did the uniforms of the island policemen. His big surprise was that with all the fancy dress, the men were barefoot. Their dark skin made the contrast a striking one, which continues to fascinate island visitors to this day.

In 1893 there was a storm that goes down in history as a terrific one. Charlie was on *Frying Pan Lightship* anchored 20 miles off shore. The wind and waves were so severe that the galley which was topside was torn loose from the deck and swept overboard. Everything was gone but the ship-mate range. It was anchored to a cement foundation, as on all ships, and there was a brass rail around the top of it so the cooking pots could not slip off during rough weather.

The crew was in a bad situation. After the storm let up the *Lightship's* steward had no pans in which to cook. There was food a plenty, stored in the hold of the ship, but it had to be cooked — salt pork and dry beans. It has been said that necessity is the mother of invention. This proved to be true with the stranded, hungry seamen. Empty paint cans were brought up from the lockers below and soon the coffee was boiling. Charlie used little strips of salt pork for bait to catch fish to go with the beans. When the meal was ready, it was truly a Thanksgiving dinner.

When Charlie was on one of the ships going into Nassau, the Captain wanted to smuggle stockings and undies in for the natives. According to the Captain, Charlie was one of the "smoothest smugglers". He would go ashore fat, his own clothing stuffed with things.

"Strange thing", the guard said to young Charlie, "you are so skinny sometimes and yet so stout at others".

LIGHT SERVICE

Charlie entered the Lighthouse Service January 1, 1894, serving as a seaman aboard the *Frying Pan Lightship*. This was no strange place for the young seaman since he had known it from early boyhood. Now he had responsibilities aboard ship. This service on the *Lightship* lasted only a short time as he was transferred to the lighthouse tender *Water Lily*.

Later Captain Henry, his father, became ill of a serious kidney disease. He was at this time caretaker of a Relief Lightship at Charleston. This ship had to be kept ready to go

Sailing vessel

out at any time to relieve other lightships in the service. Charlie was transferred off the *Water Lily* to the *Relief Lightship* to relieve his father April 29, 1897.

This lightship duty was interrupted for a short while by his service in the United States Navy during the Spanish American War, 1898. He served aboard the gunboat *USS Cheyenne* on which his half-brother George was Commanding Officer. On enlistment Charlie was made Seaman First Class and twenty-four hours later he was promoted to Quartermaster First Class. His knowledge of ships proved to be to his advantage. At the end of the War he was given an honorable discharge, having served only the last seventy days of the war. Charlie returned to the Lighthouse Service and was assigned to office duty at Charleston.

While on duty in Charleston, Charlie met Marie Rose Pozaro at the Light Station at Fort Sumpter. Bible records show she was christened Maria Rosa. She was a pretty young woman with dark hair and sparkling eyes. Her mother was Margaret Jane Whiteside, whose family was Irish Catholic from County Cork. They lived at Fort Moultrie on Sullivan's Island, just off Charleston. Her father, Charles Joseph Pozaro, years before had sailed out of Genoa, Italy, for Charleston. There he went to work on the buoy tender *Wisteria* and remained in the employ of the *Wisteria* until his death following a heart attack at the age of thirty-four. Their four children, of whom Marie was the oldest, had good educational opportunities in a Catholic school.

Charlie and Marie Rose were married October 3, 1899. They were both twenty-six years of age. There was quite a fine wedding for these two. The bride and groom had a state room on a Clyde Line steamer as he went to take over his new assignment as Second Assistant to the Light Keeper at Mosquito Inlet Lighthouse Station near New Smyrna, Florida, now called Ponce de Leon Light. They carried with them their many wedding gifts and furniture to begin their eventful life together.

Mosquito Inlet Lighthouse

During the sixty-four remaining years of Cap'n Charlie's life countless changes were to take place. There were to be many joyous, happy days and others filled with great problems, heartaches, and disappointments. A new century was beginning. They stood on the threshold of the uncharted twentieth century. Perhaps all the experiences of his active life these first twenty-six years were to fit him for the years of responsibility that lay ahead.

At Mosquito Inlet Light Station, July 16, 1900, their first child was born, a girl whom they named Margaret, for her Irish grandmother.

Two years later the Swans moved to the Little Cumberland Island Light Station in Georgia. Here Charlie was First Assistant to the Keeper. This was the same station where Charlie had lived as a boy of four to ten. However, his boyhood years were not the only time in his life that he had been on Cumberland Island.

As a young man when he was on duty on the buoy tender *Water Lily* the tender took supplies and repair crews to the Light Station. On two occasions Charlie was at the station when the President of the United States, Mr. Grover Cleveland, came down to hunt ducks.

Big and Little Islands, south of Brunswick, Georgia, have for years been considered excellent hunting grounds. Charlie paddled for the President on these hunting trips, and at the end of each hunt Mr. Cleveland gave Charlie his hunting boots to show his appreciation. These were no ordinary boots that could be purchased at any store, they were custom made for the President who had a very small foot and wore size six shoes but had large thighs. Charlie also wore size six shoes but was very slight of build. He would have been lost in the big boots had he not cut them down knee high. They were prized momentoes of the President's visits.

Both life and death came to the Swan family while they lived on Little Cumberland Island. A son and namesake was born to them, Charles Henry ("Bubba"). Captain Henry, the grandfather, who had lived eighty-one eventful and colorful years, died in Southport.

DREAM COMES TRUE

On August 31, 1903, Charlie Swan's dream came true — he was transferred to Bald Head Island! He became Keeper of the new Cape Fear Light Station on the island and had the honor of lighting the lamp to put the lighthouse into service. Captain Charles Norton Swan had reached his goal. At last he could call Bald Head Island home. He and Marie, with their two children, moved into the Keeper's new house on the island.

What is this island like? Why does it have such an appeal to those who know it best? How is it so easy for one who loves Bald Head Island to call it "my island"?

This plot of land has had many different names. Officially it is Smith Island, named for Thomas Smith, a South Carolina Indian trader. He received a grant from the Lords Proprietors on May 18, 1713, for Cape Fear Island or Cedar Island and his family owned it, or portions of it, until 1821. Because of a large, round sand dune near the river side of the southernmost ridge that looked so much like a man's bald head, the southern part of the island was called Bald Head. Those who know the place best refer to the entire island as Bald Head Island. This high dune is the first land seen by the men on ships approaching the mouth of the Cape Fear River.

Smith Island is uninhabited. It is bounded on the east and south by the Atlantic Ocean, on the west by the Cape Fear River and on the north by a series of inlets and Federal Point (Fort Fisher). The island is like a large puzzle, the many small islands making the pieces to be put together. There are three distinct ridges or islands, separated by Bald Head, Cape, and Bay Creeks. Therefore the islands, from south to north, are Bald Head, Middle, and Bluff Islands.

Bald Head is the largest and highest island. It is approximately three and a half miles long and three-fourths of a mile wide. It has a dense forest of huge live oaks (3-5 feet in diameter), tall palmetto trees, cedar, holly, and loblolly pine. Cape Fear is the point at the lower end of the island, with

Aerial view Bald Head Island. Frying Pan shoals right foreground, Cape

Frying Pan Shoals extending off shore for more than twenty miles. The exposed area of the Shoals, called the "lumps", is used as a roosting place for many birds, especially the pelicans.

The entire complex of islands covers about 12,000 acres. Of this, approximately 3,000 acres are upland and the remaining 9,000 acres are marsh and lowland. Little creeks flow in the marshes like curving ribbons.

Fear Light lower right, Bald Head Light center left, Fort Caswell across river from Bald Head. Fort Fisher and Federal Point right background

During the War Between the States Fort Holmes was hurriedly constructed (September-November 1863) on the southernmost section of Bald Head Island. Many men died of typhoid and other fevers during this time and were buried on the island. According to Cooper and Satterthwaite (*Smith Island and the Cape Fear Peninsula* — 1964) "the fort consisted of a three-quarter mile mainline of breastwork with thinner earthworks or curtain walls, revelled with oak and palmetto logs and connecting three of the five batteries, whose guns were mounted *en barbette*. Fort Holmes in the fall of 1864 mounted 15 guns, in contrast to Fisher's 47, Anderson's 11, and Caswell's 17. Those portions of the curtain outside the forest have been blown about and generally obliterated by shifting dunes in the last hundred years yet the remains of no other coastal earthwork fort in North Carolina are so extensive".

There are only a few buildings on the island today, though at one time there was a thriving little community composed of the men and their families involved with the Lighthouse Service, the Oppositon Pilots, and the Life Saving Station (now the Coast Guard). In more recent years there was, for a short time, a hotel and a pavilion on Bald Head. The lighthouse, "Old Baldy", (1817), is there near the river side and can easily be seen from Fort Caswell and Southport. There are a few deserted Coast Guard structures on the ocean side and also the three frame houses of the keepers of the destroyed Cape Fear Lighthouse.

For years *Frying Pan Lightship* lay at anchor at the end of the Shoals as a warning to ships of the danger in the vicinity. Countless ships have wrecked on the Shoals. The *Lightship* was replaced in 1964 by a $1.5 million Light Tower, located thirty miles off Cape Fear.

North Carolina's first lighthouse was built on Bald Head Island in 1796. It was replaced a short distance up the shore by "Old Baldy" in 1817. In 1903 Cape Fear Lighthouse was built and was used until the Oak Island Lighthouse was activated in 1958. (See second section of the book for stories of these lighthouses).

At Cape Fear Light Station, in 1903, in addition to the beautiful new lighthouse, there were three white frame dwellings for the Keeper and his two assistants. These houses were about 150 feet apart. There was an oil house near the lighthouse and two storehouses. One storehouse was for the Keeper and the light-

Bald Head Lighthouse

house supplies, divided by a partition. The other was for the two assistants. These storehouses were kept well stocked at all times.

All supplies to the station were transported the length of Bald Head Island. The first roadway through the island was a tramway. A flat car with metal wheels was pulled by a team of mules over the wooden rails, called stringers, set on strong, light-wood cross ties. Later the flat cars were pushed by hand.

The tramway was put down during the construction of Cape Fear Lighthouse (finished in 1903). The wooden rails were used for several years after Cap'n Charlie went to Bald Head Island. When the rails rotted, he bought old Nell, a sorrel horse, and a cart. These he used to do all the hauling that was done for all the families on the island.

Bald Head Island can not be described. Someone has said it must be experienced. Somehow on the island one feels away from the world and all its pressures. The quiet beauty of Bald Head fascinates those who are fortunate enough to set foot on its sandy shores.

Why wouldn't Cap'n Charlie love such a paradise? He did!

LIFE ON THE ISLAND

Life on Bald Head Island was never uninteresting for the young Swans who lived there. Cap'n Charlie was respected, obeyed, and loved by his children. Their mother had a wonderful sense of humor. This is a good combination for a happy home. Almost every day brought new adventures and the stories of these have been told to the children and the grandchildren of the family.

This was an unbelievable place in which the Swan family lived. They did not need modern recreational facilities — they had their own. They had miles of beaches and high, rolling dunes for their sandpile and the broad Atlantic for a swimming pool. There were many little creeks for wading and playing, and an untouched forest of thousands of acres for a park and a zoo. The children knew the beautiful birds of the island at close range, as their feathered friends. There were various species of egrets, gulls, rails (marsh hens), ibis, herons, pelicans, terns, cranes, ducks, geese, and many others. Some of these were visitors from nearby Battery Island, a large heronry in the Cape Fear River. In and out of the thick forest ran raccoons and squirrels, while on the creek banks lived mink and otter.

Day after day the young Swans learned about the ways of the wind and the rain, the seasons of the year, and the stars overhead. All the time Cap'n Charlie taught them about God as Creator.

Cap'n Charlie and the children often took long walks on the island. They went clamming together, and at night, by the light of a lantern, they went turtle egg hunting and gigging for flounder. He taught them to fish, swim, use a boat, and to cast nets to catch fish or shrimp. These nets Cap'n Charlie made himself.

By the light of a full summer moon the Swans went to the eastern beach to watch for their friend, Old Three Flipper. This female Loggerhead turtle returned from distant deep sea wandering year after year, to crawl out of the temperate waters

Louisiana Herons

of the Atlantic onto the sand beyond the high tide line toward the dunes, to nest. She dug a hole with her hind feet and laid her eggs. These 100-150 eggs that resembled dented, white ping pong balls were covered and left for the warm sun to hatch about two months later. It was easy for the Swans to know when Three Flipper came ashore because of her odd tracks in the sand. Maybe she lost her flipper in a battle with a shark.

Along Bald Head Creek, after heavy flood tides, frequently, skeletons fell out of the banks, soldiers buried there many years before during the War Between the States. The bodies had been wrapped in army blankets and buried in rough wooden boxes. As the strong winds and high tides cut into the sand banks, these boxes had fallen apart.

Atlantic Surf

On Bald Head Island it would have been easy for the Swan children to become lost, either in the dense forest, in the marsh, or in the ocean. So Cap'n Charlie had to figure out some way to let them be on their own and still be safe from the dangers that were all about them. Captain Henry, his father had used a method Cap'n Charlie decided could not be improved.

He told the children, "If you go into the thick woods alone the 'Yay-hoe' will get you". (yā-hō)

"Papa", they asked, "what is a 'Yay-hoe'?"

"Well, he's a strange creature. He lives in the deep forest and never comes out. His head is shaped like a hoe and with it he will cut your head off".

Not only did this extreme method keep the children from being lost, but it also protected them from possible attack by wild boar, snakes, etc.

"May we go on the beach and play, Mama?"

When this question came their father patiently talked with the children. "If you go alone to the water and wade out deep, there is danger. A wave might come near and a pretty mermaid say, 'Little boy, little girl, do you want to see my flower garden?' Then if you go on out into the water she'll take you to Old King Neptune in the diving bell at the bottom of the sea."

THE DIVING BELL SONG

When I was a sailor lad Some story to you I'll tell Of all the

Chorus

of the world Is down in the diving bell Down in the diving bell In

bottom of the sea Sweet little mermaids pretty little merma

All come courting me.

When I reached the bottom
I saw things that made me laugh.
They had a clothes line
Made of the Atlantic Telegraph.
Chorus
Down in the diving bell
In the bottom of the sea.
Sweet little mermaids, pretty little mermaids,
All come courting me.
Old Mother mermaid came to me
With salt tears in her eyes
Said she to me, "As you can see,
It's not fine weather to dry.
Chorus
Down in the diving bell
In the bottom of the sea.
Sweet little mermaids, pretty little mermaids,
All come courting me.
mermaid and I were married
a church of Oyster shells,

At a certain set of the tide Cap'n Charlie often went with the children to swim and play in the water, but he did not want them to go alone, even though they were all excellent swimmers.

This careful father also took the children into the thick forest. They climbed trees of all sizes. Cap'n Charlie taught them to "size up" trees, to know which were brittle and which of the cedars could be cut to get good ship knees. Cap'n Charlie liked cedars best of all the trees for this use. Knees are like the ribs of a ship with only ten necessary to make a large boat. Metal long ago replaced wood in ship building.

In all the years the Swans lived on the island, no serious accidents occurred and no bones were broken. Much of this

Forest—Bald Head Island

can be explained by the careful training of his children. E[mptied a large basin of water out the window. He]
though the young Swans were restricted and taught to prot[e]ve hit the target better if he had aimed for the w[h]
themselves against the dangers of the island they lived happ[y] In his understanding way his father forgave J[o]
lives. Their Mother's Irish wit and humor were evident in the[The only thing he could scrape off his face was di]
everyday play.

Cap'n Charlie's keen sense of humor carried

The top tower of the lighthouse was painted black because [m]any a rough spot. The crow's feet at the cor[n]
could be seen better than white. Two of the young Swans foun[d] were not altogether from being in the bright sun[
the discarded paint cans one day and there was enough pain[t] here by the crinkle of his smile.
left to give them an idea. Quickly they painted each other blac[k] In the winter by the fire or in the cool of
then went immediately to the house. When they walked int[o] [en]ing on the porch, Cap'n Charlie would sit in
their mother's room, she almost lost her breath laughing. Marie[ ]with his young children on his knee or near
called Cap'n Charlie, who fortunately was not on duty. Five[ ]them to sing the old sea chanties, some h[e]
gallons of kerosene in one big zinc tub and hot soap suds in[ ]The *Diving Bell* song was one of his fav[
another and much scrubbing by the parents removed the[ ]passed down through five generations.
paint. It was a rough scrub, however, because the children had[ ]composed by Cap'n Charlie and fellow [
unfortunately mixed much sand with the paint. At least two[ ]*Water Witch*.
Swans will never forget this paint job.

Cap'n Charlie was always one to observe rules, especially
ones that had to do with the keeping of the Light. New rules
came through that the entire station must be thoroughly
inspected each week, so Cap'n Charlie set out to keep them with
care. Each Sunday morning he had the usual family Bible
reading and prayers at ten o'clock. Then began the inspection of
the Keeper's home (his own), inside and out. After this he
inspected the First Assistant's home and the Second Assistant's
home, his next door neighbors. Beds had to be made, floors clean,
kitchen in ship-shape, and the grounds well kept.

One Sunday morning Cap'n Charlie, in his blue serge
uniform and white crown cap, was inspecting his home. He was
bent over or kneeling to look under the house. He thought he
had seen, through the lattice underpinning, a piece of paper that
had blown there.

In the upstairs, "Nutt" (John, the second son) was slipping
to use his father's straight razor to shave his thirteen year old
beardless face. Without knowing Cap'n Charlie was below, John

THE STORM S[ONG]

Stand by your halyards, bo[ys]
We have to reef her down
Frying Pan Light Ship
We will reach by mornin[g]
If our fortune favors us
Southport we will run i[n]
Unload our heavy deck[
And wait for fair win[d]
No sooner had the w[
She went down on [
Down on her beam[
The whole seas we[
The cry of the m[
And also timbers[
After killing two[
Of our devoted [

34

The Parson wore a bathing gown
The cod fish rang the bell.
Chorus
Down in the diving bell
In the bottom of the sea.
Sweet little mermaids, pretty little mermaids,
All come courting me.
We're married now and happy, too,
And living in the shade.
There's none so fair
That can compare
Although she's a mermaid.
Down in the diving bell
In the bottom of the sea,
Sweet little mermaids, pretty little mermaids,
All come courting me.

During the years Cap'n Charlie's family lived on the island, there were sometimes as many as ten children there from the families of the tenders of the Life Saving Station and the Lighthouse Service. For example, one year there were four Pinners, two Hancocks, one Smith, and three Swans.

The county, at this time, did not provide a teacher as was done later. Mrs. Lillie Burns, the mother of Edgar Burns, the Second Assistant at the Lighthouse, taught for several years while the Swans were there. They went to school at the home of Mrs. Burns. Later a little one room school was built, half way between the Life Saving Station and the Lighthouse. Miss Bertha Reed was the last one to teach in this school before all the Services were moved from the island to the mainland and school for the young was no longer a problem.

Mrs. Burns also taught a Sunday School class for the children each Sunday. She used a big picture chart and gave each child a small card with a picture and scripture verse on it. There was always good attendance and interest.

One Halloween a northeastern gale wind shrieked as the witch was riding her broom on Bald Head Island. There was a Square Dance at the Burns. They had a graphophone, an early type record player. When the young people were beginning to tire of dancing, Marie quickly cut holes for eyes in a scarf and put it over her head. She went outside to a window and knocked, when the others looked out the window they all ran to closets and hid, scared half out of their wits. Margaret hid behind the door. Her mother came to the door and opened it. There was Margaret who did not at first recognize her mother. She started saying over and over, "O, I believe in people coming back after death. I really believe in people coming back after death". Evidently Margaret was trying to be on the side of the intruding ghost.

Another trick that was a favorite on the island was to dress up a wooden ironing board like a person. A face was drawn on paper, a bonnet put on for the head, and a tippet or short cape for a wrap. The board was propped against the front door. After a knock on the door the pranksters quickly hid and watched the "visitor" fall toward the unsuspecting one who opened the door. Ghost pranks even on Bald Head!

There are those who believe to this day that the ghost of beautiful Theodosia Burr still walks on the island. Legend has it that her ghost is seen from time to time. But that's another story.

No date on the calendar brought more joy to the Swan family and the others who lived on the island than Christmas. Days ahead of time for the celebration, Cap'n Charlie went in his boat to Southport for extra supplies. Food was abundant. Fresh pork and turkeys, weighing twenty-five to thirty pounds, were cooked the day before. Cakes and pies were baked and put in the screened-in pie safe.

Bald Head Island had an abundant supply of cedar trees. The Swans went to the forest to find the best tree of them all for Christmas. They also cut holly boughs heavily laden with bright berries. Grandmother Pozaro sent a big box of decorations for the tree each year from Charleston.

On Christmas morning there was the reading of the story of the birth of Christ from the Bible and the singing of carols. Though Cap'n Charlie did not smoke or drink, he had Open House for the men from the old Life Saving Station and his own Assistants. Cake, coffee, and Port wine were served, and good cigars were given to the men. Some had to stay on watch, so the men took turns coming to visit with Cap'n Swan and his wife.

In 1911 there was a community tree for the seven families on the island and the crew at the Life Saving Station. Each person gave Mrs. Burns' daughter one dollar. She went across to Southport and bought a gift for every resident of Bald Head Island. These she beautifully wrapped and put under the Christmas tree.

When the big night arrived there was much excitement. Word was whispered around that there was an extra surprise in store, a secret that caused great speculation. The Bible story was read; there was singing followed by the distribution of the gifts. Next the grand surprise. Grandmother Pozaro had sent from Charleston a big box of fireworks! Then the fun really began.

Holidays were not the only source of entertainment on the island. A great deal of teasing went on in the Swan family all the time. An individual had to learn to take a joke to survive. The children liked to sneak into the lighthouse tower and slide down the rope that hung right in the center. The rope was used to haul the fuel up to the light and was about one hundred and thirty feet long. This was such fun and the danger of it never entered their heads. To them the greatest danger was in being caught.

Another unforgettable incident occurred the summer before Marie Rose died. One bright moonlight night Mr. Tillett, Cap'n Charlie's young Second Assistant, was on his way to take the midnight watch. The young Swans were waiting on the Storehouse porch. They had planned for days to give Mr. Tillet a scare. The bell rang for the change of watch and the children

Eastern shore Bald Head Island

flew down the hill to get in the tower. As Mr. Tillet started the long climb up the steps, they called out in strange voices, "We'll get your bones tonight". The Second Assistant took off up those steps as if he had wings. When he reached the top, he had to give some sort of explanation to the Keeper who was ready to go off watch.

"Cap'n Charlie, I don't know what's happened. Sounds like Margaret and Charlie crying."

Then it was Cap'n Charlie's time to fly down the spiral staircase. His wife was ill and of course he thought she was worse. The children had reached home before their father and had jumped into bed.

"You all right, Marie?" he asked, all out of breath.

"Yes, but are you, Charlie?"

"Where are the children?"

"In the tower I think."

Cap'n Charlie looked in their dark room and asked, "What were you doing in that tower? I'm good will to give you both a good whalin'." He always seemed to sense when the children were up to mischief.

And then there was the time they slipped into **Cape Creek** at real low water, playing like young raccoons.

"Looks deep enough to dive", someone called out.

In they went, but "Bubba" (Charlie) didn't come up, just his legs were sticking out. It was too shallow and he was stuck in the mud. The others pulled him out and washed him off, face and all.

Many happy hours were spent horseback riding. Mr. Boyd, part owner of the island at the time, had some broken down race horses and kept them on the island. The Swan children rode bareback and gave the horses plenty of exercise.

However life on Bald Head was not all play and no work. In 1911 three sailing vessels, loaded with rough cut, unfinished lumber, wrecked. All the lumber washed ashore on Bald Head Island and it could not be claimed because it was not marked.

When Cap'n Charlie was on duty and saw the rafts of lumber coming to shore; he would call to Margaret, who was then eleven and "Bubba", who was nine. They went out and dragged the lumber above the high water mark. Cap'n Charlie did this himself when not on watch. They salvaged enough lumber to put all the sub-floors in a seven room house he built on West Street in Southport, and to build a large woodhouse and a fence around the 160 x 88 foot lot. This house has stood for more than half a century and is stronger than many new ones.

Worship played an important part in the lives of the Swan children. In Cap'n Charlie's home there was always family altar before bed time. The father taught the children their prayers and verses from the Bible. After he read a passage from the Scriptures, all knelt as he led the prayer. The mother sat in a chair and the young children knelt at her knees or nearby. Up until the time the last child married this custom was observed. If the young people had guests, they were invited to join in the family altar and never was one known to refuse.

There were few, if any, dull days in the life of Cap'n Charlie on Bald Head Island; things were always happening at the most unexpected moments. His resourcefulness aided him in many an emergency.

He helped to save the wife of one of his Assistants in a very unusual way. The jealous husband threatened the woman's life.

When she knew he was coming home mad one day, she ran across the hill to Cap'n Charlie's storehouse. He was working there, but he acted as if he didn't see her as she jumped into a barrel filled with freshly picked duck feathers. Here came the husband, with a gun in his hand.

"Cap'n", he asked, "have you seen my wife?"

Calmly he answered, "No, not right lately."

Both the Assistant and his wife laughed about this later and thanked Cap'n Charlie.

On December 6, 1932, at midnight, at the change of the watch, the First Assistant Lightkeeper died of a cerebral hemorrhage in Cap'n Charlie's arms in the top of the tower. To remove the body from the tower the men made a cradle of rope (boatswain or "bos'n" type) and lowered this down the center of the tower. This was the same rope used to raise the fuel for each day.

Since his boyhood days, Cap'n Charlie had admired and treasured the friendship of Captain John L. Watts. Death came suddenly to Captain Watts on the eastern beach between the boat landing and the Life Saving Station where he had been the officer in charge for many years. Cap'n Charlie and two other men lifted his body into a boat and made the sad journey across to Southport. This trip Captain Watts and young Charlie had made together many times years before, when Charlie was with the Watts' during the summer months and gave part of his heart to Bald Head Island.

Cape Fear Lighthouse

FOOD ON THE ISLAND

Food on the Island presented few difficulties for the limited number of families who lived there year round. They raised their own cows for milk, hogs, beef cattle, and chickens for meat. Most of the beef was sold in Southport; some of it was pickled for home use, as was the pork. Fish was salted and kept, and fresh sea food was almost always available. Chickens provided eggs as well as meat. The climate was excellent for productive vegetable gardens and fruit was plentiful, especially delicious Alberta peaches. Cap'n Charlie transplanted fig bushes on Bald Head he brought over from Fort Caswell.

Flour was bought on the mainland by the barrel, sugar by the hundred pound bag, grits and rice by the peck, and canned corn by the case. There were always cured hams hanging by strong bear grass blades from hooks in the storehouse. A long black snake, which of course was not poisonous, was kept in the storehouse to keep rats out of the supplies and often could be seen hanging from the rafters.

When anyone from Bald Head Island went to the mainland for food supplies he never said he was going to buy groceries or that he was going to the grocery store. He used a much more meaningful expression, "I'm goin' across to grub up."

Cisterns were used for the water supply at the Light Station. However, three fresh-water wells were later dug on the high land near the Station.

Keeping ice on the island was a problem. Once a week it

Steamer Wilmington

was brought from Wilmington, thirty miles up the Cape Fear River. The steamer *Wilmington* had big sawdust bins in the hold of the ship for transporting it in three hundred pound blocks, tied in burlap bags. These cakes of ice were lifted over the side of the ship by a crane. At that time the steamer tied up at the old Harper dock.

Cap'n Charlie bought his ice and took it by boat to the landing on Bald Head Island. Even then he was a long way from home with his purchase, about three miles. Supplies, including the ice, were first hauled on the tramway and later in a horse drawn cart over a narrow dirt road through the dense forest.

When at last the large cake of ice finally reached Captain Charlie's home, it was kept under the kitchen in a bin of sawdust. This long journey of a cake of ice makes going to our modern ice-making refrigerators seem entirely too effortless.

Later came a wooden, metal lined, insulated ice chest where the milk could be kept cool. Captain Charlie was particular about the milk for his coffee. He did not want it kept on ice. Each warm day a little agate (enamel) bucket of milk was boiled so it would not sour. It was kept in a certain place on the porch where the breeze could blow on it.

The Swans and their friends enjoyed home-made ice cream often during the summer months, especially peach cream. This was made with the luscious Alberta peaches that grew there in such abundance.

Marie always liked to serve guests who came. She kept peaches chilled, in season, for this use. One of her favorites was cold lemonade with a few ripe peach slices in it for flavor. Marie Rose was truly a gracious hostess.

Money was a scare item in those days. On the island there was little opportunity for odd jobs and trading. Cap'n Charlie's salary was never big. Today we would say it was never adequate. What he did not have in dollars and cents, he made up for in ingenuity and resourcefulness. His pay was for years the same — $71.80 a month or — $861.60 a year. He was a good manager;

otherwise he could never have taken such care of his large family. The pay at this time for the First Assistant was $59.00 and for the Second Assistant, $45.00.

When Cap'n Charlie used his cart and Old Nell to haul groceries for the families, often they did not have the correct change. On one occasion, Mr. Burns asked Margaret, the oldest of the little Swans, to take a quarter to her father. This was a big responsibility for her, handling money. For safe keeping she put the quarter between her teeth, of all places, and ran home. On the way she thought she swallowed the money. This was a very unhappy and unforgettable day for her. Three years later, Dogney Larsen, playing up on the sand hill Margaret had crossed on her memorable monetary dash, found a quarter, maybe *the* quarter. Margaret was so filled with joy that she cried, "Come to the house and I will give you a reward". She gave Dogney all forty-three cents she had saved in her little cup. Poor business maybe, but a happy reward for both parties concerned.

Schools of porpoises play close to shore near Cape Fear

SHIPWRECKS

Many times when ships wrecked on the dangerous Frying Pan Shoals, the survivors would row to shore, guided by the Cape Fear Light. They would knock on the door of the Keeper's house. Cap'n Charlie would call, "Who is that down there?" All he needed to hear in the answer was the one word "shipwreck" and his feet hit the floor. His faithful wife, Marie, was always right with him. A quick fire was made in the Ship-Mate range (the kind used on all ships for cooking). The men would go to the Station to report the wreck, and Marie cooked ham and grits and served her good homemade bread with real butter. These things happened at all hours of day and night.

Only one time was there a woman involved in an accident at sea near the island while Cap'n Charlie kept the light at Bald Head. Years ago there was no Inland (Intracoastal) Waterway. Many yachts and small boats wrecked along the eastern coast of North Carolina.

Just before dark one evening, a Mrs. Hearst fell overboard from the yacht she and her husband were on, going from New York City to Florida. This accident happened several miles north east of Cape Fear.

Dr. Hearst threw her a life ring attached to the deck line. She caught it in the growing darkness, and her husband payed the line out enough to prevent his wife from coming into the rudder of the yacht. She must have been an excellent swimmer. The only thing they could see was Cape Fear Light. Dr. Hearst, unable to get his wife back aboard the boat because of the rough water and the darkness, steered toward the lighthouse.

He beached his boat, put her right up on the east beach, jumped out, and waded his wife ashore. He tied the yacht to a big stump on the beach. Mrs. Hearst was too weak to walk, so her husband carried her through the dark woods on the road to the lighthouse and on to the Keeper's house. He knocked on Cap'n Charlie's door. Then and there started a friendship that lasted many years.

Marie heated water in the large tub and helped Mrs. Hearst wash the salt water from her long blond hair. She gave the guest a warm gown to wear and tucked her in a comfortable bed.

Mrs. Hearst's navy blue raincoat was hung over a chair by the stove to dry. Accidentally the Swan children knocked the chair over. From the coat pocket a fabulous array of jewelry fell to the floor, diamond rings, a pin watch, and a bracelet linked with hearts. The children quickly picked up these valuable pieces and gave them to the owner.

Next day the Life Saving crew (the Coast Guard of today) and Cap'n Charlie went with Dr. Hearst in a wagon down on the east beach. By using long logs, the men rolled the yacht across the narrow stretch of beach and launched her on the creek side near Buzzard's Bay.

An interesting correspondence was carried on between these two families for a long time. Generous gifts came to the Swan family from the Hearsts in expression of their deep gratitude for the warm hospitality shown the couple in distress. At Christmas, gifts for the children came from far away New York, large dolls, a doll buggy, a small piano, tea sets, trucks, pop guns, and games.

In fair weather and foul Cap'n Charlie and his men kept the light burning brightly and maintained careful watch. During all his years at Cape Fear Light there was never a wreck in the area that was not seen first from Cape Fear Lighthouse. Flares at night curved over the horizon and could be seen from the top of the tower. Cap'n Charlie was a good spotter of wrecks, he had keen eyes for the slightest sign of trouble. The two assistants were also able men.

After a hurricane or gale, when one or more ships went ashore on Frying Pan Shoals, Cap'n Charlie notified the men on the mainland in the Pilot Tower at Southport. They, in turn, notified the tug boat company in Wilmington, and tugs were sent out to pull the ships off the shoals. Some, however, could not be moved and are there today, known as the shipwrecks off Cape Fear. This is part of the "Graveyard of the Atlantic" (David Stick).

To notify the men on shore of an emergency, a huge white flag, ten by twenty feet, was hoisted on a flag pole attached by strong ropes to the iron smoke stack of the lighthouse. A small block and tackle was used to get the flag up. Cap'n Charlie would go out on the upper deck of the tower and lash the big flag with strong sash cord. Above the flag a black canvas ball, about four feet in diameter, was also hoisted on a clear day. If the pilots on shore could not see the white flag, they could see the black ball and send assistance.

Five children were born to Cap'n Charlie and Marie while he was in service at the Cape Fear Light. These were: John Gadsden ("Nutt"), Mary Esther (Esther), Ethel Teresa (Ethel), Marie Rose (Marie), Agustus Norton (Gus). Margaret Louise (Margaret) had been born at Mosquito Inlet and Charles Henry ("Bubba") at Cumberland Island.

In 1915, when Margaret, the oldest child, was about fifteen and Gus was a baby of five months, the comparatively young mother, Marie, died of tuberculosis. This left Cap'n Charlie with seven children to care for, one of whom was afflicted and another a tiny baby.

In April of 1912 the Swan family had moved for the school months from Bald Head Island to the home Cap'n Charlie had built in Southport on West Street. This is where Marie spent her last months. Two weeks before the mother's death Mrs. Bessie Hickman had come to the Swan home to help nurse, bringing her young daughter Geneva. Afterward she stayed on as housekeeper for the Swan family.

Miss Bessie became Cap'n Charlie's second wife in 1917. Of this marriage there were born three children. One of these, Mable Brown, died in infancy. The other two were Henry Law (Law) and Reese Earnhardt (Reese). The family continued to live in Southport, except the four summer months on Bald Head. In the winter the father came to the mainland as he could, but was at Cape Fear much of the time. Miss Bessie really had her hands full with the lively young Swans.

Fish hooks play an important part in the life of a fisherman and also in the life of his family. One summer day on Bald Head Island Gus went fishing out the kitchen window, when he was just a little boy. He hooked a hog to his dismay, and Cap'n Charlie had to cut the hook out. No more window fishing.

But young Gus didn't stop there in his interest in fishing. He got his hands on one of his father's fishing lines that had a big lead and drum hook on it. Gus stood on an old box out in the back yard and went dry-land fishing again. He swung the line around his head two or three times and threw it out. Instead of catching a fish he caught a finger of his right hand with the big hook and yelled for help. Miss Bessie ran out in the yard, saw the predicament poor Gus was in, and fainted. Cap'n Charlie came running. He cut the hook off the line and used his sharp straight razor to cut the hook out of Gus's finger. A hard way to learn about fish hooks.

One day another son, Law, who was still a young boy went down to the Southport shrimp docks and got a job heading shrimp after the boats came in at sundown. The Swans were living in Southport during school months then. Law came home late. As he neared the house a neighbor said as he passed, "You'd better get on home. Your Mama thinks you've drowned and she's beside herself". When Cap'n Charlie came over from the island he talked with Law about coming in so late and worrying his mother. Law explained he was just trying to make some money and told his father that he had made three dollars.

"Well, maybe you made three dollars, but it cost me a ten dollar doctor's bill to get your Mama straight".

THE TOWER

Visitors to the Island did not have to be in distress to come to know the Keeper of the Light Station and his family. Many came across in boats to learn what the island was like. They would land near Bald Head Lighthouse and walk the three miles through the woods on the old dirt road to the Cape Fear Lighthouse. The indescribably beautiful view was worth the hike and the climb to the top of the tower. These visitors often brought picnic lunches. Many times they ate with the Swans.

As Keeper of the Light Cap'n Charlie spent many hours alone, but he was never lonely. Often the family could hear him singing from the tower, and he also had a way of whistling through his mustache that sounded like singing through a comb.

Another interest of Cap'n Charlie was keeping pets and for a while he had a pet crow and a pet raccoon. He played games during the long hours on watch to break the monotony. He would call the pigs below, "Whee, chooty, chooty. Whee, chooty, chooty". They would run about looking for him, of course with no success. He also had at least fifteen cats. From the tower he would call to them and they, too, would look for him but never find his hiding place high up above them.

Much time in the tower was spent in reading. The Light Station was furnished a library of sixty books. These, on request, could be changed every six months. Of course he had the daily papers, which came in bundles because the trips to the mainland were made about twice a week.

Keeping the Cape Fear Light was no chore for Cap'n Charlie. He had watched as it was built. As the first Keeper, he struck the match to light the kerosene lamp in the tower the day the lighthouse was put into use, August 31, 1903. This light had the reputation of being one of the best kept in the service.

For his outstanding contribution to the Lighthouse Service and his devotion to duty Cap'n Charlie was awarded the Efficiency Star while in charge of the Cape Fear Light on Bald Head Island. This award was to the Keeper of the best kept light in the district.

There was one dangerous task Cap'n Charlie would never allow an Assistant to perform — the painting of the big black ball on top of the Cape Fear Lighthouse. The entire structure had to be painted every three years. He crawled to the tip top of this 161 foot tower and painted it every time it was painted during the 30 years he was Keeper.

Cap'n Charlie tended this light from 1903 until 1933, when he retired from the Lighthouse Service. During these thirty years, the light on Bald Head Island was never extinguished, except for a period of eleven days during World War I. Then it was blacked out on orders from the Government as a preventive measure against submarine activity in the area.

During World War I there was a patrol set up on the eastern shore (ocean side) of Bald Head Island. Wooden observation towers were erected and manned from Fort Caswell, across the Cape Fear River on Oak Island. The threat of enemy submarines was far less in World War I than in World War II or than it would be now.

HUNTING AND FISHING

Cap'n Charlie was an excellent hunter. His sons take just pride in telling stories about his hunting experiences. He was a crack shot on the wing and was known to have downed nine birds with one shot. "He just didn't miss", the boys say of their father.

When he went marsh hen hunting ("marsh henning") he always bagged the limit. Cap'n Charlie did not believe in killing anything that could not be used for food, and did not kill animals or fowl just for the sport of it. He took hunting and fishing parties out and appeared to enjoy each trip more than the last one. Many hunters and fishermen tell tall tales about these times with one who had learned early in life to be an expert.

"The nicest suit of clothes Papa ever had he bought with skin money", one son said. He trapped coons right in his own garden and sold the skins. He sold the skinned coons for twenty-five cents each. A good skin brought $8 to $12, especially during the coon skin coat fad. Mink skins brought $10 to $18 and they were plentiful on the Island.

Thousands of birds follow the coast south in the fall of the year. Often they flew into the beams of the light from the tower of Cape Fear Lighthouse. Some birds were so large that they have been known to crack the glass that surrounded the lens. Cap'n Charlie sometimes buried them by the basket load. When the children were in the tower with their father he often guessed what birds hit. Bang! Cap'n Charlie would say, "That's a duck". He knew how to interest the young Swans in everything about them and was constantly teaching them. Many tiny rice birds flew into the light and were blinded by it. When they hit the tower they were instantly killed by the impact. These Cap'n Charlie and the children gathered up and picked the feathers off each one by hand; they were like little butter balls. Marie made a delicious pot of stew of rice birds, onions, and rice. Birds without hunting!

> "The sea bird wheeling round it, with the din
> Of wind and wings and solitary cries,
> Blinded and maddened by the light within
> Dashes himself against the glare, and dies."
>
> (a verse from Longfellow's *The Lighthouse*)

Cap'n Charlie was hunting alone on Bald Head at the Smokehouse Pond at Cape Creek on Bluff Island. He shot the ducks and went out to get them. As he walked he went deeper and deeper in the mud. He thought he could not get out and decided to stick his gun up in the mud to mark where he went down so those searching for him could find his body. As he did so his gun hit oyster shells. This was solid and Cap'n Charlie pulled himself out. Never too old to learn!

Each fall Cap'n Charlie enjoyed fishing alone for spots. He cast his gill net off Caswell beach at low tide. This fisherman had learned while quite a young boy to make these beautiful, strong nets. The fish were caught in the net by their gills. He usually caught enough spots for himself and his married children to salt down for the winter. Many times he had a surplus which he sold for his catch was sometimes as much as three hundred pounds.

RETIREMENT

When the calendar pages finally turned to the time Cap'n Charlie was to retire from his responsibility as Keeper of the Light — *his* Light — the date was April 1, 1933. He had served twenty nine years and nine months at Cape Fear Light Station on Bald Head Island, and ten or more years at other stations. His successor was Captain James Smith, followed by Captain Munn, at whose retirement the Coast Guard took over the responsibility of manning the Light Station.

But surely no other man could possess this structure as Cap'n Charlie did. It was steel and concrete, reaching one hundred and sixty-one feet to the sky and sending its light in a radius of more than 18 miles, to aid the men on the ships at sea. But to him, Cape Fear Light was almost a living thing and he treated it as such. To leave the Light was perhaps the most difficult assignment he had in all his years in the service.

Cap'n Charlie had to learn to be retired, as do most men. But he was resourceful and the many interests he had developed during the years came to his aid. He had to be busy to be happy, and he had a family to support. The word soon got around that he was available for house painting and carpentry work; he was an excellent cabinet maker. The Cap'n did these odd jobs about town until he was eighty.

Cap'n Charlie Swan was a devoted Christian. He was a member of the old Trinity Methodist Church in Southport. He and his family had a regular pew, and he was president of the Men's Bible Class.

After Cap'n Charlie's death, William Williams, principal of the Southport High School, presented a Bible to the class in memory of their devoted president. Inscribed in the Bible were the familiar words Cap'n Charlie used every Sunday at the close of the class, "Everybody come again next Sunday and bring somebody with you".

He not only worshipped regularly in the church each Sunday, but his loyalty was demonstrated during the week by the way he lived and the things he did for the church. He used his talents to good advantage. Cap'n Charlie knew how to beautify the grounds and keep up the building, and this he did.

Trinity Methodist Church is one of the oldest churches in the area. It is a beautiful, small, white frame structure and stands on a quiet street surrounded by tremendous old live oaks. As the sun shines through the stained glass windows they lend an indescribable beauty to the high ceiling and walls of stained wood.

After Cap'n Charlie was seventy years old he painted the entire church. For his work he would not accept a penny; this was his service to the Lord.

One unhappy day, while painting the church, he lost his balance on a high ladder and fell to the ground. For weeks he was in the hospital. This gave his many friends an opportunity to show their affection and appreciation to Cap'n Charlie. The visitors were many, and his room was kept filled with flowers. Cards and letters came in a steady flow bringing deep joy to this quiet, humble man.

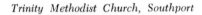

Trinity Methodist Church, Southport

Cap'n Charlie also helped with the upkeep of the small local Dosher Hospital. All his work there was his gift. He did not have millions of dollars to give to the world, but what he had he gave, kindness, friendliness, and his talents.

Jimmy Harper said of his friend: "Cap'n Charlie dignified simple goodness. Some think it's simple to be good — Cap'n Charlie changed this in the minds of many."

Bald Head Island has often been used by the U. S. Military for survival and landing maneuvers. The forest is so dense and the terrain so similar to other sections of the world that it serves this purpose well.

For many years Reese, Cap'n Charlie's youngest son, has been the keeper of the island for its owner, Mr. Frank O. Sherrill. Part of the time he stays in the old Cape Fear Lighthouse Keeper's dwelling. Otherwise, he stays with his wife and children in Southport. Like his father before him, Reese had come to know and love Bald Head Island from his early years. The entire family still thinks of the Island as their second home.

Reese was informed about landing maneuvers that were to take place at Bald Head and asked Cap'n and Miss Bessie if they would like to go over to watch. Five to eight hundred men were on the island from Fort Eustis, Virginia. This was to be a practice supply movement. Forty men of the opposition were to try to keep the men from coming ashore in various landing craft.

On the river side of the island the three Swans, plus Reese's faithful Labrador, Lee, tied up the boat in which they had crossed over from Southport. They got in the International Scout (a type of jeep) furnished Reese for use on Bald Head. The Swans were on the front seat with Lee riding in the back. They headed for the woods road, which is like a narrow tunnel through a dense jungle.

A shot rang out just before they reached the far edge of the forest where the camp was located. Lee lunged into the front seat and scared the Swans as much as the shot, which was a

Road through forest on Bald Head Island

plenty. The shot was a blank fired by the security guard, as a warning that someone was approaching. Brakes were jammed on and the three, or the four counting Lee, were put under arrest. At least one of the forty men was really on the job. After a full explanation and a check with the officer in charge, the "captured spies" were released and became the honored guests for the practice run. Cap'n Charlie especially enjoyed every minute of this experience, that is, except the shot in the dark forest.

This event occurred in 1961 and it was said that the maneuvers were interrupted by the Cuban crisis, some of the men being sent directly from Bald Head Island to the trouble zone.

Cap'n Charlie had few aids to travel during his ninety-one years. Each one had a particular place in his life. His horse, old Nell, and the cart were used for years on the island. He, like all others, used a sail boat and the paddles for a long time. He crossed over to Southport from Bald Head Island with the tide, and a good wind brought him back home.

About 1906 Cap'n Charlie bacame the owner of the first motor boat in the area, the "Commander Rogers". This boat served between the days of the sail boat and a later cabin cruiser.

There was only one car in the long life of Cap'n Charlie. This came late in his life and brought him much enjoyment.

His son "Nutt" was home on leave off a dredge. He bought a second-hand car, just to have something to run around in while ashore. It was a touring car, a 1925 Chevrolet. This model had wooden spokes in the wheels and curtains, kept folded under the back seat, that could be put up on the sides in case of rain. There were small "windows" of isinglass in the curtains, a brittle plastic-like material. The car had running boards and fenders. At the end of his leave, "Nutt" asked his father if he would like to have the car. What a gift! Of course Cap'n Charlie accepted the challenge. He went to the City Hall and bought his first driver's license, no examination required in those days. This purchase started one of the most remarkable driving careers ever known in the quaint little village of Southport.

Being accustomed to a boat all his life, he handled his new conveyance in the same manner. He would open her up full speed, either going ahead or astern. The starter broke soon after he began driving, and Cap'n Charlie never had it fixed. He said he could crank it just as well by hand, maybe better. When he cranked her, she would either be in or out of gear, little difference he said. He hopped in, headed the front end in the direction he wanted to go, and stepped on the gas. It was full steam ahead!

Often he'd load the children in the car, his kin and others in the neighborhood. He would take them the short distance of a few blocks to the Amuzu Picture Show, operated by Mr. Price Furpless. All who could get in the car did so for the excitement of the ride. No one was happier than the pilot of the car.

But one night her brakes didn't hold very well, and Cap'n Charlie over shot his mark. He took her over the curb and sidewalk right into the side of the entrance of the Amuzu. Bricks were knocked out of the building but not the high spirits of the laughing, uninjured passengers and the driver.

A sturdy garage was built at the end of the side drive at the Swan's home. Cap'n Charlie spent many hours building this cover for his prized possession. Several times, when he stepped on the gas to get through the sand in the driveway, he went right on through the back of the garage. He finally put an 8 x 8 timber at the back of the building to serve as a bumper.

He talked to his car the same way in which talked to his boat; this was most of the time. Cap'n Charlie had been on watch alone at the lighthouses so much that it was natural for him to talk to himself some. After the timber was down, he stepped back, looked at his car and said, "I reckon that'll stop you."

Miss Bessie would hear him coming down the quiet, tree lined street. She'd call to the children, "Get out of the driveway, Pa's coming in with the car." One word of warning was enough and they scattered like sand fiddlers on the beach.

About twice a year Miss Bessie and the children would go to Wilmington (thirty miles away) to shop. Cap'n Charlie would drive them to the ferry slip on the Brunswick county side, but he would not cross the ferry in the car. What a blessing! He set the time he'd meet them at the ferry, and they were always there without fail.

Finally the engine of the car wore out. Cap'n Charlie gave away what was left and never drove again. No one can understand how it held together as long as it did. In his life the car was like a brilliant shooting star. While it lasted it was sheer joy to the retired Keeper of the Light.

Cap'n Charlie owned a house-boat that he moored at Bluff Island in Cape Creek on Bald Head. This boat had a stove and space for four to sleep. After his retirement he often camped out there alone or with some of his family and friends. They fished and hunted, had oyster roasts and fish fries. Here they recalled other days on the island in years gone by. Somehow the island changed very little with the passing of time.

There was one possession of Cap'n Charlie's that took first place over all others. This was a trim cabin cruiser named for his first wife, *Marie Rose*. Mr. Gibbons, from upstate, had the cruiser built. He was at the time part owner of Bald Head Island, with Mr. T. F. Boyd.

After his retirement Cap'n Charlie was caretaker of the boat for about five years. Then he bought her from Mr. Gibbons, fixed her up to his own liking, and enjoyed this excellent boat for many years.

The *Marie Rose* was about twenty-five feet long and could sleep four people. She was painted white with a varnished house and green deck. The name was proudly displayed in bold letters on both bows and the stern.

Cap'n Charlie could do almost anything with that boat. Once after a bad huricane, he paddled her in the dark, without lights of any kind, from the yellow banks to the Yacht Basin. He and the *Marie Rose* actually felt their way along the marsh and came on in. This was almost a miracle. Had he missed the way he would have gone out to sea. The Cap'n was very strong physically, though he was a small man in stature.

Not only did Cap'n Charlie enjoy this boat but the entire family did. He often took friends or guests in Southport to Bald Head Island on turtle egg hunts or on fishing trips.

One summer four young women were spending their vacation on the coast. They went to the dock at Southport and asked a short man, wearing a white top cap, if he knew anyone who could take them over to see Bald Head. At once Cap'n Charlie smiled and said, "I can and here's my boat, the *Marie Rose.* Ready to go?"

As they crossed to the island, their pilot talked of his years on Bald Head as Keeper of the Light. They sensed how he missed the responsibility of the lighthouse. He seemed so happy to take interested visitors to the spot on earth he knew so well.

He put the girls out to walk to the Cape Fear Lighthouse through the forest on the narrow woods road. On the way they found a little lost dog that they added to their party, so now there were five hikers.

Soon the leafy green tunnel ended, and there on the sand were three white frame houses not far from the ocean and, to their amazement, young men in uniform. They thought Bald Head was uninhabited! One of the men said in a rather stern voice, "Where did you four women come from and where did you get our dog?" All four started explaining at once, and the dog joined in with happy yelps at being home again. When an acceptable explanation was given, one of the Coast Guardsmen climbed to the top of the lighthouse tower with them for the breathtaking view at early sunset. He took them back to the river side of the island, to save them the long walk through the dark forest. This was a flying trip in a stripped down jeep. They reached the beach and no Cap'n Charlie was in sight. The driver of the jeep just sat and looked at them and his eyes were asking, "What was the real story?" Then they remembered the man had said if the tide changed he would be at another place at a certain time and there he was.

The girls sat on the flat bow of the *Marie Rose* and with Cap'n Charlie at the wheel, went into the sunset toward the mainland. They rode in silence, awed by the beauty all about them, the sky, the sea, the island, and by their pilot, Cap'n Charlie Swan.

Geneva, Cap'n Charlie's step-daughter, and her family were devoted to him. Many times after his retirement, Geneva left her household duties to go on trips with him so he would not have to go alone. They lived on the Yacht Basin and her sons grew up around Cap'n Charlie. He taught them the lessons of the sea, even as he had taught his own children many years before on Bald Head Island. They learned to steer a boat and learned the ways in and out the creeks of the marsh. Later one of the boys, Bob Smith, became a Cape Fear River pilot of large ships, as had one of Cap'n Charlie's own sons, "Nutt."

An even more constant companion than his grandchildren was a faithful dog named "Gyp" (Gypsy) that went everywhere with Cap'n Charlie. She was a good swimmer and loved the water. The dog was sent from California by Law and was a pedigreed, jet black Labrador retriever — a large, long-haired dog. "Gyp" died when she was about ten years old, and her master really grieved for her.

DEATH AND BIRTH OF A LIGHTHOUSE

Cap'n Charlie lived long enough to see the lighthouse he loved so dearly die. He outlived it by about six years.

Because the authorities believed the Cape Fear Lighthouse should no longer stand after the new Oak Island Light was activated, May 15, 1958, it was destroyed September 12, 1958. There was the danger that seamen might mistakenly take a daylight fix on the tall Cape Fear tower. It was therefore considered a "menace to navigation."

Cape Fear Lighthouse was a steel skeleton tower and proved to be difficult to demolish. Several delays were necessitated by its excellent construction.

The day before the tower was destroyed, Cap'n Charlie went over to Bald Head Island with a few members of his family. He went into the lighthouse for the last time. Moving pictures were made of him as he left the lighthouse. He turned and touched his white top cap, as a farewell salute to the tower.

The following day, in the early afternoon, several of the Swans watched from across the bay at Southport. They heard the explosions and saw the large cloud of dust and sand that rose skyward as the structure toppled to the ground. Cap'n Charlie could not look, the lighthouse was too much a part of him. The blast seemed to tear his heart out.

After over half a century of service Cape Fear Lighthouse was condemned. The light last burned May 15, 1958. On this same date Oak Island Light was activated.

Even as Cap'n Charlie lived to see one great light extinguished, he also lived to see another even brighter light put into service. He had lighted Cape Fear Light in 1903 and now he was given the honor of lighting the new Oak Island Light — the brightest in the nation.

This was a high day in Cap'n Charlie's life. Many dignitaries were present for the activation ceremony on May 15, 1958. Rear Admiral H. C. Moore, Commander of the Fifth Coast Guard District, was the principal speaker. Several others participated in the ceremony before James C. Bowman introduced Captain Swan by giving a review of Cap'n Charlie's career in the Lighthouse Service. Then he added:

"During his life he has witnessed the transition from beacons that used hog fat as fuel, where it was necessary to burn an alcohol flame under the fat during the winter months to preserve its liquid form. Since then lights progressed to the point where they used kerosene. From there to lights that burned as a result of the discovery of electricity. Today we have this light that has been developed to the point where it generates 14-million candlepower and is the brightest light ever maintained by the United States Coast Guard.

"It is only fitting and proper that this new light which we are dedicating today be actuated by Captain Swan."

With dignity, eighty-five year old Cap'n Charlie, dressed in his spic-and-span dark blue serge uniform and white crown officer's cap, stepped to the speaker's stand and, in a quiet voice, acknowledged the honor that was his. These are the notes he wrote for this important occasion —

I deem it a great honor to have been chosen selected to throw the switch that put in operation another new lighthouse.
And I want to express my sincere appreciation to Adm Moore and other officials of the U.S. Coast Guard, as well as other friends for this great honor. It has made me very happy indeed.
May this light proove to be a blessing to those who go down to the sea in ships and a guide to those in the air,
I thank you

Then Cap'n Charlie pulled the switch that brought life and light to Oak Island Lighthouse. Long may it shine in all its brilliance!

Rear Admiral H. C. Moore, Commander of the Fifth Coast Guard District and Captain Charlie Swan

JUST SITTIN'

During his eighty-fifth year Cap'n Charlie's activities became limited because of rheumatism in both legs. They had carried him far, but now his pace was slowed down. He used a walking cane. Even then he hobbled (to use his term) across the hill to see and touch his beloved boat, the *Marie Rose*. He could not take the boat out for about two years before his death. Much of his time was spent *just sittin'*. He sat many an hour on the brick wall down on the Yacht Basin, watching the ships as they went up and down the Cape Fear River and out on the broad Atlantic.

Surely during these hours Cap'n Charlie relived the days of his young life at sea and the years that followed.

The last year of his life he sat every day, morning and evening, on the steps of his comfortable white, two-story, green shuttered home in the shade of the large live oaks. This was the house on West Street in the construction of which years before he had used lumber salvaged from the wrecked ships near Bald Head Island.

People passing waved to him and called out their greeting. His presence on the water front was sorely missed. Countless hours he had sat on the weather worn Whittlin' Bench at the dock, swapping tales with other "Old Salts." When someone asked how to find Cap'n Charlie the answer was often, "Look down by the water for the short little man with a close cropped mustache and a white top cap."

The neighborhood children all visited with their beloved friend as he sat on the steps of his home. One of the joys of these last years was the loyal friendship of his next door neighbors, Tillie and her family. Many stories of the sea were told to his young visitors, whom he seemed to enjoy even more than those of his own age.

This is one of the ways through the years the rich traditions of the courage, daring, and adventures of the men of the sea have been passed from generation to generation.

One afternoon when Cap'n Charlie was about eighty-eight he was sitting in the sun on the front steps of his home. Jimmy Harper walked by and stopped to pass the time of day with his admired friend. Being a newspaper man, Jimmy has ears for a newsworthy story and he heard one that day. The conversation rather naturally turned to fishing. Fish were not biting good that week, except Bonito.

"Most people don't care for Bonito, but I do," Cap'n Charlie said, "because they once saved my life. It was the year before I went into the Lighthouse Service. That was back in 1893, nearly seventy-eight years ago. I was making a trip from Haiti to Boston on a two-masted square-rigger, and we ran out of food. All except flour, and the cook we had made good bread.

"One day while we were becalmed (this means there was no wind for their ship's sails), we saw a school of Bonito swimming around the bow of the boat, and we rigged a harpoon to try to spear one of them. The cook called us to supper, and I just didn't want to go down and eat any more dry bread. I decided to try one more time with the harpoon. I did and hit one. I had a time with him, but finally I got the fish aboard. The men heard the fight and came running up to help. It weighed about a hundred pounds, and for three days we had fish and bread.

"We had run out of grease, so all the cook had to fry the fish in was scrapings we had saved from the galley to use in greasing the mast. There was a little paint oil in the can, too, but that didn't ruin the fine flavor of our fish. By the time it was gone we had reached the Pilot boat at Boston harbor, and they let us have some grub.

"What people have against Bonito is that they have red meat. They taste all right. And even now I eat one every once in a while to remind me of how thankful I was to get one when I thought I was going to starve to death."

The day Cap'n Charlie was ninety years old there was a great celebration. According to the local newspaper, the *State Port Pilot*, the entire town joined in. To quote the *Pilot* of .August 21, 1963:

"The first phase came Sunday morning when the members of the Men's Bible Class at Trinity Methodist Church paid tribute to their oldest and most faithful member. Captain Swan has been president of this body for several years.

"At the eleven o'clock worship service Captain Swan was joined by almost all the members of his immediate family, some from out of town, and they filled almost three pews in the sanctuary. The Rev. Chas. Lancaster spoke for the congregation in extending best wishes to Captain Swan.

"The birthday observance continued during the afternoon when Captain and Mrs. J. I. Davis (Esther Swan) held Open House. Scores of friends called to speak to Captain Swan and to express their best wishes on the anniversary of his birth."

Few live to be ninety, and few individuals pack as much real living into their allotted years as this man did.

Another quiet year rolled past for Cap'n Charlie, and now he was ninety-one. This birthday was observed in the home place on West Street. Again the family he loved so devotedly came; about fifty-five descendants were present. Esther baked and decorated a birthday cake with candles for the gathering. The minister of Trinity Methodist Church was invited to join the Swans.

Some of the members of the family were at sea, but in their hearts they were in Southport. This is a close knit family and all will remember Cap'n Charlie's ninety-first birthday as long as they live. They knew he was "living on borrowed time," but what they could not know was that in less than two months he would be gone.

THE BAR

On Saturday morning, September 5, 1964, Cap'n Charlie suffered a stroke which caused him to lose the entire use of his right side, and he also could not speak. This made it very difficult for him to communicate with those who nursed him and with his family. He was taken to Dosher Hospital immediately and died there three weeks later, two o'clock, Sunday morning, September 27. Cap'n Charlie died in his sleep. Two of his sons were with him.

Services were held Monday afternoon at his beloved church. Three ministers participated in the simple but beautiful service, Rev. Chas. H. Lancaster, Rev. L. D. Hayman and Rev. Edward B. Jordan. By his request, Mrs. Rachel Rook sang "Let the Lower Lights be Burning." The burial was in the Old Southport Cemetery. The remaining family were his wife, Mrs. Bessie Swan, five sons, five daughters, many grand- and great-grandchildren.

CROSSING THE BAR
Sunset and evening star,
And one clear call for me!
And may there be no mourning at the bar,
When I put out to sea.
But such a tide as moving seems asleep,
Too full for sound and foam,
When that which drew from out the boundless deep
Turns again home.
Twilight and evening bell,
And after that the dark!
And may there be no sadness of farewell,
When I embark;
For tho' from out our bourne of Time and Place
The flood may bear me far,
I hope to see my pilot face to face
When I have crossed the bar.

Pallbearers were members of the Men's Bible Class of Trinity Methodist Church. Expressions of condolence came from those in both high and low estate. Numerous florals and memorials were sent to express sympathy to the family and to honor this respected man. By his request his white top cap was buried with him, held in his right hand, over his heart as if at salute. Also by his request, Tennyson's *Crossing the Bar* was read by a former paster, Rev. Hayman.

Surely Cap'n Charlie left his footprints not only on our shores but on the sands of time.

The lead editorial of the *State Port Pilot*, September 30, 1964:

Captain Charlie Swan

"Southport lost another of its flavorsome characters this week with the death of Captain Charlie Swan, surely one of the most beloved citizens of this community.

"If you were to ask what made Captain Charlie such an outstanding citizen, it might be a little hard to explain. He wasn't rich, he never sought or held public office, he was not a business, social, or educational leader. The three dominant forces in his life were his church, his family, and fishing.

"But more than any man we have known, Captain Charlie gave dignity and meaning to simple living and good moral conduct. He had an abiding faith in his fellow man and he never liked to dwell too long in conversation about those who had failed to measure up to the mark.

"He led the good life, and in the living was an inspiration and an example for those who knew him. It is a sad commentary upon our times that there are so few men like Captain Charlie Swan left in this world."

Captain Charles Norton Swan
Keeper of the Lights!
May the memory of your life on earth,
Be passed from generation to generation
Of those who love the sea.

The United States of America
honors the memory of

CHARLES N. SWAN

This certificate is awarded by a grateful nation in recognition of devoted and selfless consecration to the service of our country in the Armed Forces of the United States.

Lyndon B. Johnson
President of the United States

72

Lights

of the Lower Cape Fear

Cape Fear

Moseley's Map—1733

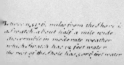

LIGHTHOUSES

For centuries lighthouses have been used by mariners as guides. These structures, displaying a light or lights, have varied in form, material, height, and durability. The lights have varied in strength from burning coals to lights rated at more than a million candle power with coded flashes, attaining many miles of visibility.

"In the earliest lighthouses, centuries before the Christian era, the light came from a brazier of burning coals hung from a pole. As far back as the 7th century B.C. there was a lighthouse at Cape Sigeum on the Asiatic side of the Dardanelles. The most famous lighthouse of antiquity was the tower built on the island of Pharos in the day of Alexandria in the 3rd century B.C. This was considered one of the Seven Wonders of the World, and for a long time the name "pharos" was given to all lighthouses. At Boulogne, on the French side of the English channel, the Romans built a great tower 192 feet around and 200 feet high, which guided mariners for more than 14 centuries."[1]

"The first lighthouse in America was built in 1716 on the site of the latter-day Boston Light. Before that only bonfires or burning barrels of pitch on headlands guided ships to port at night. Shipwreckers would duplicate the crude beacons on lonely stretches of coast to lure ships onto the beach where they could be looted.

"The earliest lightship station was that at Craney Island at Hampton Roads, Va., where a decked over small boat was moored 1820. The first outside lightship was stationed at Sandy Hook in 1824.

"In Colonial times, aids to navigation were built and maintained by the various localities. The responsibility for aids was taken over by the Federal Government in 1789, when the Lighthouse Service was established in the Treasury Department. The Service was under Treasury's Revenue Marine Bureau (1845-

[1] Reprinted with permission of the copyright owner, F. E. Compton Co., division of Encyclopaedia Britannica, Inc., Chicago, Illinois.

74

1852) and the Lighthouse Board (1852-1910) which passed to Commerce in 1903. The Service was a Commerce Bureau (1910-1939) until returned to Treasury and the Coast Guard.

There are now over 39,000 navigational aids — lighthouses, buoys, fog signals, radio beacons — which the Coast Guard maintains. More than 500 of them are fully manned lighthouses".[1]

Operation of these many aids is easier today than in the days when the light was made by tallow candles and lamps burning fish oil, sperm oil, colza (oil from wild cabbage seeds and other plants) and lard oil. Kerosene in various forms proved to be quite satisfactory. Electricity has cut the cost of maintenance because care is less and fewer keepers are required.

"Some present-day lights and fog signals are turned on and off by a remote radio control system called ANRAC (aids to navigation radio controlled). There are other electric wonders: RACON (radar beacons) which give distance (up to 120 miles) and bearing of ships and planes from the beacons, and LORAN (long range aids to navigation) which provides navigational information to air and surface craft".[1] These modern methods are a great improvement over the use of burning coals in a metal container hung from a pole out toward the sea or the use the mariners made of the salt works on the North Carolina shores to guide them in.

There have been many aids to navigation through the years along the North Carolina coasts. The lights of the Lower Cape Fear River have served sea faring men in this area from the first lighthouse that was put into use on Bald Head Island in 1796 to the most recent one erected on Oak Island in 1958.

Longfellow, in the last lines of the poem *The Lighthouse*, speaks for all lighthouses:

> " 'Sail on!', it says, 'sail on ye stately ships!
> And with your floating bridge the ocean span;
> Be mine to guard this light from all eclipse,
> Be yours to bring man nearer man!' "

[1] The Public Information Division of the United States Coast Guard, *Coast Guard History*.

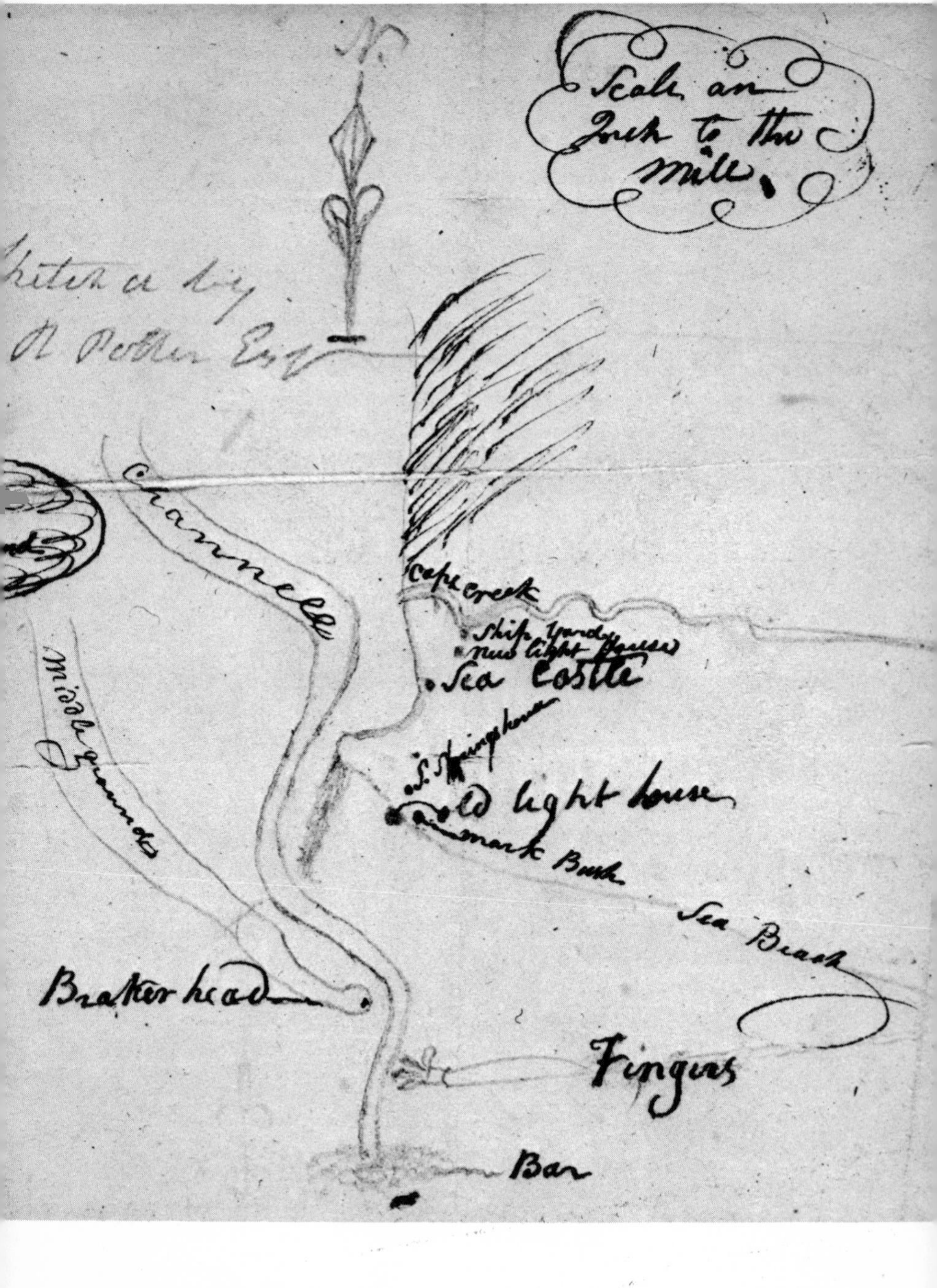

N

Scale an Inch to the mile

Sketch a by
R Potter Esq

Channell

Cape creek

Ship Yard
new light House

Sea Castle

S Springhouse

Old light House

mark Bush

Middle grounds

Sea Beach

Braker head

Fingurs

Bar

Anomymous engraving—Frontispiece in a religion book (published 1817)
"View of a Water Spout at Entrance Cape Fear River"

BALD HEAD LIGHTHOUSE

In 1784 the General Assembly of the new state of North Carolina levied a duty of six-pence-per-ton on Cape Fear shipping to finance a lighthouse on Smith Island, at the mouth of the Cape Fear River. Before the responsibility for the aids to navigation was assumed by the Government in 1789, the communities involved built and kept the aids.

Building this lighthouse was not an easy task. Disaster was experienced at every hand. In *Southern Architect*, September, 1963, Dr. Louise Hall wrote: "From the beginning it seemed a hard-luck project. Nothing went right. Vessels carrying brick to the island became stranded in the shoals, the master-builder died possessed of other materials for its construction, and the tower remained unfinished in 1789."

When the Lighthouse Service was established in the Treasury Department, under Alexander Hamilton, there were twelve colonial lights in operation between New Hampshire and South Carolina and four incomplete projects, one of these being Bald Head Lighthouse.

On December 14, 1790, the State of North Carolina ceded to the United States ten acres, which Thomas Smith's great, great grandson, Benjamin Smith, had given to the state for a lighthouse site. On April 2, 1792, Congress appropriated $4,000 to complete the project begun eight years before. Three further appropriations totalling $7,359.14 were made between 1793 and 1797. The light was completed and first shone in 1796, according to the Coast Guard Information Division. Some set the date a year earlier.

"During 1792 and 1793", to quote Dr. Hall, "at least three cargoes of brick were shipped down from Philadelphia at the order of Tench Coxe, U. S. Commissioner of the Revenue, and on March 30, 1793, Abishia Woodward of New London, Conn., master-carpenter, contracted with the government to superintend completion of the lighthouse for 'four Dollars and two-thirds of a dollar per day". The Cape Fear masons and bricklayers were paid 'One Dollar and one third per day'.

"The spring of 1793 President Washington appointed as general supervisor of the project, George Hooper of Wilmington, a Massachusetts-born merchant. Mr. Hooper procured large quantities of lumber and lime. The shipment of Philadelphia brick reached the island in bad condition. There were many problems connected with the construction."

Abishai Woodward arrived from Connecticut, also the iron lantern, the Boston glass, and the whale oil for the lamps. In the National Archives is his manuscript, dated January 10, 1794, giving Woodward's 'Directions for Putting up the Lantern to the Light-house at Bald-head.'

"On December 5, 1794", according to Dr. Hall, "the lighthouse was completed and read for use. Henry Long was appointed first Keeper and was paid the highest salary in the lighthouse service at that time — $333.33 and his dwelling.

"The light was burning 'very clear' by March 2, 1795, when Hooper forwarded to Coxe new 'Directions for the Masters of Vessels bound to the Port'. Under these circumstances, the official date of 1796 for the first Bald Head Light becomes rather less than 'very clear' today".

In *Smith Island and the Cape Fear Peninsula* (1964) Arthur W. Cooper and Sheafe Satterthwaite wrote: "On May 21, 1810, Albert Gallatin, Secretary of the United States Treasury, had authorized an expenditure of up to $2,000 for two double rows of poles driven and filled between with brush, in order to secure the lighthouse at Baldhead against the encroachments of the sea.

"This is evidence that severe erosion occurred on the island's extreme southwest shore, where the 1796 lighthouse stood. This shore might have been severely eroded sometime during the War of 1812, making a replacement necessary. Only an early steel engraving of a waterspout approaching the lighthouse remains to give any idea of the first lighthouse on Smith Island".[1]

Joshua Potts of Smithville, wrote on August 24, 1813: ". . . the Shoals to the Southward of the Light House have been much altered, and the Light House itself is now washed down, by the gradual encroachment of the Sea on that part of the Land. In mean time, a point of Sand shoal has been formed a little below the place where the Lighthouse stood, and which has of late, made an angle to the westward in the channel, which was formerly straight".

"Reference was made in newspapers of seaport cities in connection with proposals for bids for the erection of a new lighthouse to the bricks and the 'old lanthorn, which is understood to have sustained but little injury in the taking down'. Obviously it had not fallen down", Dr. Hall reports.

Since the exact details of the last days of the old lighthouse are not known, we can only put together the conclusive evidence that the cause for a need to replace Bald Head I was erosion of the shore on which the lighthouse was built and the increasing encroachment of the sea.

For twenty years or so this first lighthouse on the Lower Cape Fear was the guide to the ships coming in with their cargo. Although much progress has been made in the power of the beams that go out from the modern lighthouses, the same courage and loyalty were required in 1796 as today — perhaps a more rugged courage. Bald Head Lighthouse was indeed a worthy predecessor to all the lights that have followed.

BALD HEAD LIGHTHOUSE
("Old Baldy")

On April 27, 1816, Congress appropriated $16,000 for building the replacement of the first Bald Head Lighthouse. The light was known for many years as Cape Fear Lighthouse, as Smith Island was called Cape Fear Island. The 1845 Light List says the elevation of the light above the sea at high water was 110 feet, visible 18 miles.

The Treasury Department on May 22, 1816, published in *The National Intelligencer* of Washington, D. C., the following:

"Proposals will be received at the office of the Commissioner of Revenue for building a Light-House on Bald Head in the State of North Carolina, together with a dwelling-house, of the following materials, dimensions and description:"

Then followed detailed specifications of the proposed lighthouse. It was to be built of hard brick, octagonal in shape, the foundation of stone was to be laid as deep as necessary and to be carried five feet above the surface of the earth. The wall to be seven feet think. The diameter of the base from the bottom of the water table to the top thereof, where the octagonal pyramid is to commence, to be thirty-six feet, and the diameter fourteen feet six inches at the top or floor of the lanthorn. The water table to be capped with hewn stone at least eight inches wide, and sloped to turn off the water. From the surface to the top of the building the walls to be ninety feet in height and graduated from five to two feet thick.

Minute instructions as to how the top was to be constructed were given. The platform on the arch was to constitute the floor of the lanthorn and to be of marble or freestone, and to project beyond the walls fifteen inches. The ground floor was to be brick and the other floor, as well as joists and stairs, to be of Carolina yellow pine clear of sap. A window was to be in each story, of sixteen panes of glass, ten by twelve inches, in strong frames well painted. On the lower floor a substantial panel door, three feet by five and a half. The outside of the pyramid to be rough plastered and the inside rough pointed. The doors, sashes, window frames, etc. to be well painted.

Bald Head Lighthouse (1817)

The bricks were to be "all sound and of the best quality, and the work to be well bound, and good lime mortar used throughout". Then the Proposals go on to verify for all time a frequently disputed matter, the fact that this was to be the second lighthouse on Bald Head or Cape Fear Island.

"There has been saved from the old Light House, and cleaned, a large number of sound bricks, variously estimated at from three hundred and fifty to six hundred thousand; and there remains likewise the old lanthorn, which is understood to have sustained but little injury in taking down. These are to be taken by the contractor."

The bids for construction of the new tower were opened in July, 1816. Daniel S. Way's bid was low. He had not visited the island, so he had not examined the total picture.

Mr. Way arrived in December and soon learned something of the enormous task that lay ahead. According to Joshua Potts, who is quoted in Dr. Louise Hall's article on "Old Baldy" in *Southern Architect*, Mr. Way did not know the new lighthouse

would be built about a mile up shore. This would necessitate the "large pile of old bricks being removed from the bold shore approximately a mile, over a shoal of five feet of water, to the new site, a small distance up the mouth of a creek, and thence by land a few rods to the place of the intended lighthouse".

First the contractor built the keeper's house for temporary quarters for the workmen. The directions for the dwelling call for it to be of brick, thirty-five feet by seventeen feet, one story high, ten feet pitch, with a gable end roof. The walls were to be twelve inches thick and a good brick chimney was to be built at each end of the house, with a suitable fire-place in each room.

The house was to be divided into two rooms of equal size with a passage between, leading from back to front and good double floors throughout. Walls and ceiling were to be plastered and whitewashed. Two shed rooms to be built in the rear of the house of equal size, divided by a piazza (porch), and also a piazza to be built in the front, the entire length of the house.

Bald Head Lighthouse and Robert Gaskins buoy tender dock

83

When the dwelling was completed Mr. Way started the erection of a lighthouse that stands today, one hundred and fifty years later, "Old Baldy". It is, according to records, the oldest lighthouse on North Carolina's shores.

In 1866, after a new light had been built at the New Inlet entrance of the Cape Fear River to replace Federal Point Lighthouse, Bald Head Light was extinguished. It is recorded that this was the third light on almost the same location, the second one having been burned during the War Between the States.

In 1880, however, Federal Point Light had been rendered useless and was discontinued because of the closing of New Inlet channel by the construction of "The Rocks". Bald Head Light was relighted and together with a small stake light on the beach in front of it, served as a guide through the sixteen to eighteen foot Oak Island channel across the bar, according to the United States Coast Guard.

Erosion became the difficult problem for "Old Baldy" in 1881. Two years later to prevent the lighthouse from destruction, a stone jetty 150 feet long was authorized for the protection of the foundation of the tower. Two years after this the jetty was extended another 50 feet.

Because Bald Head Light was so far inland and was not of sufficient height to light the dangerous Frying Pan Shoals, the Board recommended a first-order lighthouse, with a radius of 18½ miles light and about 150 feet high, be built on the southeastern tip of Smith Island. This new skeleton tower was completed and was activiated August 31, 1903. At this time the old Cape Fear Station (Bald Head) was changed to a fourth-order fixed light and its name officially changed to Bald Head Light Station. It was discontinued in 1935 and a radio-beacon was established on the site in 1941. This beacon was of service during World War II when Fort Caswell, across the river, was used by the U. S. Navy.

Art Newton wrote of Bald Head Light: "The old tower enjoys the distinction of being able to serve shipping in a more modern way since its light has been darkened. Operating as a radio beacon Bald Head can direct a modern ship into the channel in thick weather when even the new light (Cape Fear) may be obscured". When Oak Island Light was activated on May 15, 1958, the Oak Island Station took over the operation of the radio beacon that had been at Bald Head.

Today "Old Baldy" stands as a beloved reminder of the past. It is a landmark that has stood and served for a century and a half (1817-1967).

Cap'n "Sonny" Dosher in doorway of Bald Head Lighthouse

Cape Fear Lighthouse

CAPE FEAR LIGHTHOUSE

In 1903 a new lighthouse was added to the service. "Old Baldy" (for years referred to as Cape Fear Light) was no longer capable of meeting the needs of the ships coming into the Cape Fear River past the dangerous Frying Pan Shoals.

According to the Coast Guard Information Division, in 1889 the Lighthouse Board recommended a fourth-order lighthouse, with a radius of 18½ miles of light, about 150 feet high and costing $150,000 to be built on the pitch of Cape Fear. By 1893 the estimate had been revised downward to $70,000. On July 1, 1898, Congress appropriated $35,000 for the new lighthouse, with authority to contract for another $35,000, followed by an appropriation of a similar amount on March 3, 1901. A new skeleton tower was completed in 1903 on Smith Island and furnished with a first-order flashing lens apparatus.

The new light was built near the southeastern end of Smith Island at Cape Fear, where Frying Pan Shoals begins and extends 20-30 miles southeastward into the Atlantic. It was impossible to put building material ashore at the location selected for Cape Fear Light Station. The contractor made and carried out ingeneous plans to meet this problem.

Mr. Johnny Potter of Southport (born 1884) worked on the building of this Station and remembers vividly his experiences there. A big barge loaded with lumber anchored close to the beach at Bald Head Lighthouse. Men pushed the lumber overboard and Johnny Potter, Joe Arnold and Charlie Rourk swam it in one piece at a time. They, shoved it to shallow water and men waded it ashore where other workmen built a dock. They started on the beach side and built as far out as possible, then pile drivers finished the job.

This, however, was only the beginning. The new lighthouse was to be built abou three miles away, so a road had to be cut through the thick, jungle-like forest to the other end of Bald Head Island. Here the forest is said to resemble the way it was 400 years ago when the white men first came to the Cape Fear region. Some live oaks measure 3-5 feet breast height. The undergrowth is heavy and matted. After the oak, palmetto, cedar, pine and yaupon trees were cut to clear the way for the road, the stumps had to be dynamited out of the ground. Mules and heavy machinery were used to scrape down the hills and level the road bed. An old building, perhaps a pilot's house, had to be moved and under all the rubbish there were countless rattlesnakes.

A track was laid on the road of stringers or wooden rails, resting on heavy cross ties; this was called a tram road. Men unloaded the building material from the barge on to the dock and others loaded it on the iron wheeled flat cars that were pulled on the tram road by a team of mules to the site of the new lighthouse.

The foreman, Mr. Rob Weeks of Southport, and the contractor, Mr. Pollard, stayed on the beach in a small temporary house, the other workmen came over daily by rowboat from Southport. A work day started at sunup and lasted until sundown. The fifteen year old water boy was paid 50c a day and all laborers got $1 a day.

It was summertime when the road was cut through to the construction site, so the workmen were bothered by the heat but much more by the swarms of mosquitoes. Everyone brought his own lunch and a barrel of fresh water was hauled to the island each day. A quart of molasses was put in the water to "help the men keep going, otherwise they would pass out". The only other water was surface water near Bald Head Light. At this time Cap'n "Sonny" Dosher kept "Old Baldy" and lived in the keeper's house, though his family lived in Southport. The lighthouse was built and also three houses for the keepers and their families, the store houses, oil houses, etc.

Cape Fear Lighthouse was not constructed of brick and sandstone, as the two previous lighthouses on the island. It was a steel skeleton tower, enclosing a stair cylinder or inner tower. The entire structure was painted white, and the upper part was later painted black, beginning with the watch-room balcony, so that it could be seen more easily.

The Cape Fear illumination apparatus rotated on a mercury float. The light was incandescent oil vapor, using a 6 inch wide mantle, with a lens that was six feet in diameter and ten feet in height. The light had a 160,000 candle power that was visible 19 miles. According to the List of Lights, a United States Government publication, this light was 161 feet high.

Certainly the lantern is the heart of any lighthouse. The lantern-room at Cape Fear Lighthouse had two solid brass portholes. The lens was run by weights on heavy cable which the keeper had to wind every three hours; there was a big brass handle for this use. The keeper also had to light the mantle at sundown and turn it off at sunup. There was always danger that the lantern would become flooded with fuel oil and the important schedule delayed. The lantern had to be throughly cleaned after each time it burned to keep the light at maximum power. The watches were from sundown to midnight, from midnight to sunup, and so on around the clock.

Cape Fear Light was set burning by Cap'n Charlie Swan, who was given this honor as first keeper. He tended the light for thirty years and only two men followed him for brief periods of service before the Coast Guard took over the keeping of Cape Fear Light and the radio beacon at "Old Bady".

Because of economy and efficiency of operation Cape Fear Lighthouse was replaced by Oak Island Lighthouse May 15, 1958, and was demolished September 12, 1958. The steel tower proved to be a stubborn victim of a wrecking crew, requiring a second charge of dynamite to topple her to the ground. According to the *State Port Pilot* of Southport: "Statistics on the wrecking job indicate that a total of 62 sticks of dynamite were required to bring down the sturdy structure. The first shot tore away four of the eight supporting legs and still it stood. When the final shot came witnesses say the tower 'went down like a tall, slim tree'.

"It is ironical that on Tuesday night, the day following the destruction of the old light, trouble developed with some mechanism of the new light, which failed to function properly for several hours."

The three keeper's houses were left and later used by the Coast Guard until all services were moved to Oak Island. The houses are there today and one is used by Reese Swan who keeps Bald Head Island for the owner Mr. Frank O. Sherrill and is on the island a great deal of the time.

Before the blasting of the light tower the valuable lens, the three ton turn-table, and other parts of the light had been removed. This was a difficult task because of the weight of the apparatus. The purchaser and workmen carefully took the lens

apart, one screw at a time. They realized this was too beautiful a thing to damage or destroy.

At the time of this writing the lens of the demolished Cape Fear Lighthouse is understood to be in a Wilmington warehouse. Perhaps one day it can be brought "out of mothballs" and put at Southport for visitors to see. Rumor has it that the lens was exhibited at the World Exposition in Paris the same year the Eifle Tower was first shown. No verification through the Mariners Museum for this can be found, though the years fit perfectly.

"Cape Fear Lighthouse, a tower of steel and masonry that withstood the ravages of time and the elements for 55 years" is today only a thing of history. In the hearts of those who knew and loved this light it is a treasured memory.

Site of Cape Fear Light Station. Keepers' dwellings left—"Old Baldy upper right

Oak Island Lighthouse in process of construction

OAK ISLAND LIGHTHOUSE

Cape Fear Lighthouse on Bald Head Island was replaced by the modern Oak Island Light near the southeast point of Oak Island on May 15, 1958. It marks the entrance to Cape Fear River and is maintained by Coast Guard personnel. This was the first light to be built in the Fifth Coast Guard District (Maryland, Virginia and North Carolina) in 54 years.

The tower is 169 feet above water and its light can be seen nineteen miles. The List of Lights records the top of the lantern 155 feet above ground. Under normal (good) conditions the light's intensity is 1,400,000 candle power. When visibility drops under 12 miles the candle power can be increased to 14,000,000. The light tower, a cylindrical concrete structure with its top third black, middle third white and lower third gray, was constructed by W. F. Brinkley and Son, of Granite Quarry, North Carolina. The color was mixed with the concrete so that painting will not be necessary.

The *State Port Pilot* of Southport, December 25, 1957, reported:

"Residents of this area were treated to both a spectacular air show and a view into the future of construction methods Wednesday when the new lighthouse on Oak Island was fitted with the lens protection assembly suspended from a hovering Marine Corps helicopter.

"The air lift was made necessary when the construction crew found itself "painted into a corner". With the 148 foot supporting structure completed, it was found that the only means of installing the protective framework at the top was to set it down in place from above. Coast Guard officials put through a call to the Marine Corps, which graciously loaned two large HR2S helicopters for the job.

"The lantern, which had been shipped from Portsmouth aboard the Coast Guard cutter *Narcissus,* was attached to the hovering aircraft, piloted by Major R. D. McKitric, USMC, and was lifted into position above the tower. After some jockeying, necessitated by high winds, the assembly was lowered into place and secured by construction worker W. T. Dennis.

"The operation was not only hindered by the elements, but also by the fact that Major McKitric could at no time see where he was placing the framework. In this he was helped by the other pilot, Captain W. E. Corley, who radioed maneuvering directions to the lifting aircraft.

"Among those covering the operation were representatives from the Associated Press, International News Service, Life Magazine and WMFD-TV."

On May 15, 1958, the new Oak Island Lighthouse was ready to be put into service and was activated at a ceremony attended by a large number of visiting dignitaries including Rear Admiral H. C. Moore, Commander of the Fifth Coast Guard District.

The *State Port Pilot* reported that Admiral Moore described the new light as the most powerful operated by the United States Coast Guard and the second most powerful in the world. The most brilliant is a light operated by the French on the English Channel.

Lt. Commander C. S. Rojeski, commander of the Coast Guard Group in Wilmington, served as Master of Ceremonies. The invocation was by the Rev. Lawrence Bridges, pastor of Trinity Methodist Church in Southport and Mayor E. B. Tomlinson, Jr., of Southport spoke briefly. As James Bowman introduced Captain Charlie Swan, he recalled interesting highlights of Captain Swan's career in the Lighthouse Service and paid tribute to his loyal efficiency.

"On August 31, 1903, he kindled a spark that produced a light at Cape Fear Light Station on Bald Head Island and for almost 55 years this light has been a symbol of safety and friendliness to those of us who go down to the sea in ships . . . It is only fitting and proper that Captain Swan actuate this new light that is to replace the Cape Fear Light."

After Cap'n Charlie acknowledged the honor that was his, he threw the switch that put in operation another new lighthouse, the brightest in all the land.

"The Oak Island Lighthouse not only will replace Cape Fear Lighthouse but will also serve as a radio beacon navigational aid, a function now performed by the old Bald Head Lighthouse."

In the informative and interesting magazine, *The State,* for October, 1966, Paul Pleasants writing about Oak Island Light said: "Eight lights are in the top of the tower, half rated at 140,000 candlepower; the other four with 1,400,000 candlepower.

"The lights come from mercury arc bulbs, operating at 480 volts each, and behind each is a 30-inch reflecter. While they have a life expectancy of 200 hours' service, sometimes they will blow after only a few hours' service. And according to regulations, when one bulb fails, all the others must be replaced at the same time. When you figure the bulbs cost $400 each, it is easy to see that guarding our coast is no trifling expense.

"The Oak Island's signal is four flashes at one second intervals; then six seconds of eclipse. The flash effect is achieved because the lights are mounted on a circular track.

"The blinding heat of the high intensity lights makes it necessary for a man to wear protective clothing while working on them. And even with this protection, a man can stay in the beacon room only a short while.

"Incidently, the Oak Island light is a lot 'taller' than it appears to be. The builders went down 125 feet before finding a rock foundation, and here is where the construction commenced. Sturdy as it is, it sways as much as 3 feet in a 60 mile gale, and was designed to do so."

Oak Island Lighthouse (1958) and Coast Guard Station

FRYING PAN LIGHTSHIP

Apprehension concerning the possibility of strong hurricane force winds blowing the Frying Pan Lightship from her moorings helped to bring about the decision to relieve this light vessel, as well as several others.

"On Tuesday, November 27, 1964, the Frying Pan Lightship sounded a whistle salute to her successor, a new light tower. This Lightship was established in 1854. So, after one hundred and ten years of warning ships away from Frying Pan Shoals, the Lightship was replaced by a new off-shore Coast Guard light station, the first of three such structures to relieve three light vessels in the district.

"Ceremonies aboard the station designated the beginning of operation November 27, and at this time the Frying Pan Lightship circled the new tower and bade farewell to the waters she had guarded these many years. A series of blasts from the lightship whistle marked her departure for Morehead City for a brief stay before sailing for Cape May, New Jersey, where she serves as a relief lightship".[1]

Sprunt, in *Cape Fear Chronicles,* wrote in 1914 (50 years ago): "Light Vessel Number 94 was built for the station on Frying Pan Shoals, in the sixth lighthouse district. The vessel was 135 feet 9 inches over all, with a beam of 29 feet and a draft of 12 feet 9 inches; the displacement of this draft is 660 tons. The hull is built of mild steel with two wooden deck-houses on the spar deck serving the purpose of pilot-house and bridge-and-radio house. One steel lantern mast of diameter sufficient to contain a ladder giving access to the lantern, and a wooden main mast carrying a fore-and-aft sail are fitted. The signal light is carried on the lantern mast. It consists of an incandescent oil-vapor light mounted in a lens of the fourth order, and gives a light of 2,900 candle power.

"The complement of this vessel is four officers and ten men. The officer's quarters, mess-room, pantry, and bathroom are located as far as practicable on the main deck. Quarters for

[1] Star-News Newspapers, Wilmington, N. C.

the crew, including the galley, are located on the main deck just forward of the boilers and machinery. The oil room and stores are located on the lower deck and in the hold forward and aft. The hull is yellow, with "Frying Pan" in large black letter on each side. Construction was commenced on May 28, 1909. On November 15, 1911, the light vessel was placed on the station in the sixth lighthouse district".

This vessel of which Mr. Sprunt wrote was not the first nor the last vessel in service on Frying Pan Shoals, but is typical of the complete accommodations required for the Lightship. Even this vessel did not have electricity and those in use earlier were much more limited in the "comforts and conveniences of home".

Neither Bald Head Light nor Cape Fear Light could send their beams to the extreme end of Frying Pan Shoals. To navigate the Cape Fear River safely, the masters of ships must know where the end of the spit is located. For many years 12 miles off Frying Pan Lightship a buoy has marked the end of the broken ground and other danger spots in the area.

Crossing the Cape Fear bar today is quite different from what it was during "the blockade running days, when there were no lights or buoys, nor any guide save the lead, the line of breakers, and possibly an outline of shore".

The Lighthouse Service Bulletin of August 1, 1930, reports on the problems concerning the placing of Frying Pan Lightship. On July 16 of that year the vessel was moved 14 miles southeasterly from its previous position and moored at the southeastern extremity of the 10-fathom curve. At its previous position it was only 3 miles from the 18-foot curve. On the same date a regular radio beacon was established on this lightship. The gas and whistling buoy was placed at the old station.

The changing of the position of the Frying Pan Lightship has through the years been a matter of grave concern to those involved. The new position put it about 5 miles outside of any sounding less than 6 fathoms. It was originally established in

1854 near the former position (about 10 miles inside of a 5½-fathom sounding). The Lighthouse Board in 1907 moved the lightship near where it was placed July 16, 1930. This action aroused such local opposition that in an appropriation for a new lightship in 1908, the Congress specified that it be placed at the former inner station. The Congress also added a stipulation that the lightship could not be moved "from the place designated for its station in the act authorizing its construction".

When the new lightship No. 94 was completed in 1911 it was placed at the inner position. The lighthouse administration did not deem it necessary to maintain two lightships so close together. The subject arose again about the need of a radio beacon in the area, but not at the inner station because "vessels steering for it in fog would be brought too near the dangerous shoals. Also reports from the master, of experiences during recent hurricanes passing up the coast, showed that the lightship was anchored too near the 18-foot curve for the safety of the vessel and the crew".

The question had been under discussion for 23 years. The move on July 13, 1930, to the outer station, with the addition of a valuable radio beacon, put the lightship in a position to be of greater service to vessels of increased draft and speed.

The new lightship on Frying Pan Shoals was No. 115, a modern vessel and "the first lightship on the Atlantic coast with Diesel electric propulsion, and all its signals are electrically operated. The radio beacon operates for fifteen minutes out of each hour in clear weather, and continuously during fog; the electric light is now of 16,000 candlepower".

However all this was eventually not sufficient aid to the traffic of the Cape Fear River and the Frying Pan Lightship has been replaced. Some have the dream that one day the Frying Pan Lightship may come "home" to Southport and drop anchor there. Then visitors could tour this brave little ship that guarded the dangerous waters so long.

FRYING PAN LIGHT STATION

The Frying Pan Light Station was constructed in 1964 by McDermott, Inc., Harvey, Louisiana. The deck house was built in Morgan City, Louisiana, and brought on a huge barge to the Frying Pan Light Tower site. The six room house was lifted from the barge by a tremendous crane to its location on the foundation of steel. This type structure is sometimes referred to as a Texas tower.

The workmen for this job stayed in Southport during the Station's construction. To see them take off early each morning in a helicopter from the parking lot at the City dock (near the old Whittlin' Bench) was like seeing giant bumble bees at work. The whir of the 'copter's propellers became a familiar sound there during these months. The workmen went about their tasks as if they were building an ordinary house on the side of a hill.

"Although the new light station is intended primarily as an aid to navigation, there also is oceanographic equipment aboard.

"Located twenty-eight miles southeast of Cape Fear, the station is manned by a crew of six Coast Guardsmen who spend two weeks on duty and one week on liberty.

"Work on the station, which cost approximately two million dollars, was begun at the site in August, 1964. Its four main steel legs, driven to a depth of two hundred and ninety-three feet below the ocean floor, hold the twenty-five foot high, five hundred and fifty-five ton deck house, which is thirty-six feet square.

"A tower above the deck house houses two twenty-four inch rotating beacons of 3.5 million candle power which may be seen for 17 miles at sea. The fog signal emits a three-second blast every 30 seconds and can be heard for six miles.

"Designed for a 75-year span and for maximum resistance to wind and wave action, the station may be switched to automatic operation should it become necessary to remove the crew in case of a direct hit by a hurricane.

"The Frying Pan Lightship was a familiar sight that will be seen no more; but whether it be from a shiny new off-shore station or a time-and-weather worn ship, sea farers will ever welcome a beacon in the dark and an eerie blast on a foggy night. Someone is waiting up to see them safely into port".
(Star-News Newspapers, Wilmington, N. C.)

Frying Pan Light Station (1964)

FEDERAL POINT LIGHTHOUSE

On the southernmost point of Fort Fisher there have been three lighthouses. The Federal Point Lighthouse was a guide for ships entering New Inlet. There was a small Pilot's Beacon down the shore which aided the pilots guiding their ships through the Inlet. This may have been referred to in some cases as New Inlet Light. It is altogether possible that both names, Federal Point and New Inlet, referred to the same light.

Federal Point was named during the early 1790's in honor of the Federal Government and the ratification of the United States Constitution by North Carolina in November, 1789. In 1861 the Confederates changed the name to Confederate Point — a name which was changed back to Federal Point upon the Union victory in 1865.

The first lighthouse was erected in the months between September, 1816, and March 1817, under the supervision of Robert Cockran, Collector of the port of Wilmington. The cost of construction was $1,300. The *Wilmington Advertiser* on Friday, April 22, 1836, reported: "The Beacon at Federal Point was destroyed by fire on the night of Wednesday the 13th instant".

This first lighthouse was replaced by one begun in July, 1837, under the supervision L. H. Marstellar, Collector of the port of Wilmington and it was completed December, 1837, at a cost of $4,845. Additional construction was done on the second lighthouse between August and November of 1838, costing $750. This appears to have been a more pretentious structure. According to 1849 records in the Library of Congress, it contained 11 lamps with 14 inch reflectors, a fixed light with visibility of 15 miles. The height of the tower from the base to the lantern was 40 feet. A complete renovation of the lighthouse and the keeper's dwelling was made during the years 1843 through 1845. It is recorded that this second lighthouse was burned during the War Between the States in 1863. The encroachment of the sea has washed away the ruins of this lighthouse tower, but the foundation of the keeper's dwelling can be seen today in an area called "Battle Acre" at Fort Fisher State Historic Site.

Despite the fact that all lights were extinguished at the advent of hostilities between the States in 1861, Colonel William Lamb found it necessary to have a beacon at Fort Fisher mounted on a very high mound of earth called Mound Battery, to guide the blockade runners through New Inlet. The beacon was only lighted upon the return of the proper signal from a friendly vessel and, after the vessel had entered the Cape Fear safely, the light was extinguished. From reports, this light was a type of mobile unit.

After the Civil War, a third lighthouse was constructed in 1866 and remained in use until 1881 when the New Inlet, which had opened in 1761, was closed by a stone dam called "The Rocks", built by the United States Army Engineers. The ruins of this lighthouse are still in existence and perhaps will someday be uncovered for visiting by the public.

Price's Creek Lighthouse (1850)

A CHAIN OF LIGHTS

PRICE'S CREEK LIGHTHOUSE

On August 14, 1848, the Congress of the United States passed an act appropriating $6,000 for the erection of two beacon lights, placed in the best manner, at Price's Creek, Cape Fear River, N. C. In the same act appropriations were made also for beacon lights on the Cape Fear River along the upper jetty, Campbell's Island, Orton's Point, and on Oak Island and for a light boat to be located at the Horse Shoe, between New Inlet and Price's Creek.

(Excerpts from Lighthouse Records and the *Wilmington Chronicle*, Wednesday, September 6, 1848)

In a recent paper on Price's Creek Light, William G. Faulk has gathered interesting and valuable material concerning this chain of lights, with special attention to Price's Creek, the only remaining tower of this group built 1848-1851. •

"Located on the west bank of the Cape Fear River near Price's creek, about 2 miles above Southport, N. C., is an abandoned lighthouse tower and nearby, the ruin of the light keeper's dwelling house. This tower is visible from the Southport — Fort Fisher Ferry as it approaches. The beach in front of the tower remains today much as it did 100 years ago."

In the Price's Creek paper Mr. Faulk says of James Sprunt's *Tales and Traditions of the Lower Cape Fear*: "This publication was given to Captain Harper, owner and master of the steamer *Wilmington* and was used by passengers as a self-explanatory guide book while going down the Cape Fear". The little book pointed out Price's Creek Lighthouse and keeper's residence, telling of their use during the Civil War as a signal station.

"Price's Creek Light House — Confederate States Signal Station. We see on the Western side the old ante-bellum light house and keeper's residence on Price's Creek, which were used during the Civil War as a signal station — the only means of communication between Ft. Caswell at the western bar and Fort Fisher at the New Inlet via Smithville, where the Confederate General resided.

"The Confederate States Signal Corps frequently rendered some very effecient service to the blockade runners after they had succeeded in getting between the blockaders and the beach, where they were also in danger of the shore batteries until their character became known to the forts.

"As the signal system developed, a detailed member was sent out with every ship, and so important did this service become that signal officers, as they were called, were occasionally applied for by owners or captains of steamers in the Clyde or at Liverpool before sailing for Bermuda or Nassau to engage in running the blockade.

"The first attempt to communicate with the shore batteries was a failure, and consequently the service suffered some reproach for a while, but subsequent practice with intelligent, cool headed men, resulted in complete success, and some valuable ships, with still more valuable cargoes, were saved from capture or destruction, by the intervention of the Signal Service, when owing to the darkness and bad landfall, the captain and pilot alike were unable to recognize their geographical location.

"To Mr. Fredrick Gregory, of Crowells, N. C., belongs the honor of the first success as a signal operator in this service. Identified with the corps from the beginning of the blockade, and with the Cape Fear at Price's Creek Station, which was for a long time in his efficient charge, he brought to this new and novel duty an experience and efficiency equalled by few of his colleagues and surpassed by none. It was well said of him that he was always ready and never afraid — two elements of the almost unvarying success which attended the ships to which he was subsequently assigned . . . ."

(Tales and Traditions of the Lower Cape Fear
   James Sprunt, published in 1896
   Reprinted by permission Laurence Sprunt)

The Price's Creek Lighthouse was contracted to be 20 feet high, built round of hard brick on as deep a foundation as necessary. The base was to be 17 feet in diameter and that of the top 9 feet. Walls were 3 feet thick at the base, graduated to two feet at top.

The iron lantern was to be sufficient for six lights 24 x 15 inches in each octagon. The lantern to be fitted up with eight lamps and eight 14 inch reflectors.

Robert G. Rankin, Collector for the port of Wilmington and Superintendent of Lights, stated that no piling would be required at Price's Creek site and that the ground was too low for cellars. He recommended that the "Keeper's house be put on the site of the back beacon with tower on it, same as at Orton's Point and Campbell's Island".

In a letter of July 31, 1850, Mr. Rankin wrote to the Collector of Boston for the annual supplies of oil for Orton and Campbell's Island and on the 23rd of July had written for supplies for the new lights at Price's Creek. On August 23 Mr. Rankin nominated Zachariah Jackson as keeper of the Orton Light and Mr. John Bell as keeper of the beacon at Price's Creek.

In a letter of May 2, 1851, from Mr. Rankin:

". . . I also enclose you an acct. of Mr. Wm. A. Wright, for services rendered under the appropriation for the erection of Light Houses etc.

"The Special accts. alluded to in my letter of 25th. April were of —

1st Jany. 1850 for erection of Beacons at Oak Island
1st May 1850 Aug. 17/50 for erection of Beacons at Orton Point
1st May 1850 Aug. 17/50 for erection of Beacons at Campbell's Island
21 Jany 1851 Aug. 17/50 for erection of Beacons at Price's Creek

An interesting P. S. added at the lower left of the page of this letter read; "The Light Boat has arrived".

A later annual report of the Lighthouse Board reported:

"Two beacon lights: one 35ft and the other 25ft in height. Range lights for channel; lighted Jan. 21, 1851. High light in wooden tower on keeper's house. Keeper's house brick.

"Beginning with the 1863 Light List these beacons were listed as extinguished and after the War Between the States in 1867 they were listed as "not re-established". These lights were never relit after the Civil War."

The restoration of Price's Creek Lighthouse and keeper's dwelling would indeed be of interest to North Carolinians who cherish the history of the state.

ORTON'S POINT AND CAMPBELL'S ISLAND LIGHTS

Orton's Point and Campbell's Island Lights were apparently constructed on the same plans as Price's Creek, also the keeper's dwellings. Today Campbell Island is known as Big Island and is eight miles south of Wilmington. The lighthouse foundation may be seen there today.

The Lighthouse Letters from the Archives supply informational material regarding the countless problems, reverses and adjustments in the building of necessary lights for the increasing traffic of the Cape Fear River.

HORSE SHOE LIGHT BOAT

A Letter from Mr. Rankin, 2 Jany. 1850:

". . . the passage around the Horse Shoe is difficult and narrow and the *Light Boat* is intended as one of the chain of Lights extending from the Jettys and is from its intended position, considered one of the most important — in fact from my knowledge of the river, I would consider those at Price's Creek almost useless without the Boat".

Foundation ruins Campbell's Island Light

OAK ISLAND LIGHTS

The two Oak Island Lights were apparently the first built in this interesting chain of lights. They were first lighted on Friday, September 7, 1849.

The Wilmington Chronicle, Dec. 13, 1848, printed from the Collector's office of Wilmington:

"Proposals — by 16th. day of January, finding materials and building two Light Houses to range with the channel on Oak Island, and dwelling house, of the following materials:"

Then followed a 600 word detailed description of requirements for the construction of the two lighthouses. They were almost identical with the Price's Creek directions. There were two round brick towers at Oak Island — the high and low lights. They were clearly marked on an old military map. There was no light on the keeper's dwelling. The first Light was to be 20 feet high. The second Light was "to be built in all respects like the above, except it is to be carried up thirty feet instead of twenty and to be placed a suitable distance from it, and with the latter to range with the channel in entering the Cape Fear River".

There were instructions concerning water. "A well to be sunk sufficiently deep to procure good fresh water at a convenient distance from the dwelling house, bricked or stoned up, with a curb, windlass, chain, and bucket, or if water cannot be had by a well, then a suitable sized cistern to be built".

Because the dwelling house for the keeper and his family at Oak Island Lighthouse was apparently much like all others built in this chain or at this time, there follows a detailed description of the house. Instructions were that the dwelling was to be placed a convenient distance from the two towers. This information is from the published proposals in the newspapers.

"The Dwelling House to be of hard brick, 34 feet by 20, one story, of eight feet high, divided into two rooms, with an entry between, the stairs to be in the entry, to go into the chambers, which are to be lathed and plastered — a chimney, near the middle of the home, with a fireplace in each room,, iron or stone pieces, cellar under whole of the house, with sufficient walls of brick laid up in lime mortar.

"The roof to be rectangular, the boards of which to be jointed and halved, and well secured and covered with good interchangable shingles — three windows in each room of sixteen lights of 8 x 10 glass each, and one of the same dimensions in each chamber. The doors to be paneled, with good hinges and thumb latches to each, and a good lock on the outside door. Closets in each room back of the chimney — all of the floors to be double and well nailed, the inside walls and ceilings to be lathed and plastered, and all the inside work to be finished in a plain and decent style, and with good seasoned lumber.

"Also a porch or kitchen, attached to the dwelling house, 14 x 12 feet in the clear, 8 feet high — the room to be lathed and plastered, with double floors, two windows and one door — a chimney with a fire place and sizable oven with an iron door — crane, trammels and hooks in the fire place in the porch or kitchen — one side of the chimney a sink, with a spout leading through the stone wall.

"All the woodwork inside and out to be painted with two coats of good paint. Gutter to lead round the house with spouts to carry off the water — an out house of brick, five feet by four, the roof shingled and painted.

"The two towers and dwelling to be completed in a work-man-like manner on or before the 1st day of September next.

"No payment to be made until the buildings are completed, inspected and approved.

Dec. 13, 1848

Wm. C. Bettencort
Col."

Nothing is left of these two towers today as far as is known. The 1859 Light List describes the Oak Island Light Station as having 2 brick towers surrounded by sand hills designed to serve as range for crossing the Oak Island Bar.

The 1866 report says "A keeper's dwelling with light on top has been erected at Oak Island".

It is supposed that this dwelling was built immediately after the War Between the States to take the place of the 2 destroyed brick towers until the more permanent and perhaps stronger light could be established on Oak Island. This presumably was the Light Station referred to sometimes as Caswell Light but on Light Lists as Oak Island Station.

These range lights on Oak Island, Price's Creek, Orton Point, and Campbell's Island all had a high light and a low light. At all except the two on Oak Island, the high light was in a tower erected on the roof of the keeper's dwelling.

The procedure for the ships approaching these lights was to come into range where one light was above the other and then the Masters of the ships could be certain they were in the proper channel.

The chain of lights was a valuable aid to ships coming into the Cape Fear River through New Inlet. After the construction of "The Rocks" in 1881 and New Inlet was closed, this chain of lights was not as essential to navigation into the Cape Fear, and the beacons were not rebuilt after the War Between the States.

Keeper's Dwelling—Price's Creek Light

"THE OLD LIGHTHOUSE," PRICE'S CREEK, SOUTHPORT, N.

Oak Island Range Light   (Caswell)

OAK ISLAND RANGE LIGHT
(Caswell Light)

Very little is known today about an interesting range light that was located on Oak Island off the road to the left of the present Fort Caswell gate. Many know this as the Caswell Light, although it was listed as Oak Island Light Station.

It is possible that the two earlier range lights (high and low) on Oak Island (1850) were destroyed during the War Between the States and that this "gingerbread-type" wooden frame tower on a brick base was later constructed to meet the needs of ships entering the Cape Fear River. New Inlet was closed in 1881 and all traffic entered through the mouth of the river. The United States Coast Guard publication on Lighthouses says, "The range lights on the upper jetty of Cape Fear River, which had been installed in 1856, were extinguished by the rebels in 1861, and the structures entirely destroyed". It is supposed that the range lights on the lower Cape Fear met the same fate. Only the ruins of Price's Creek Lighthouse remain of all the range lights of this period. The foundation of the range light on Campbell's Island or Big Island (1850) may be seen today.

The wooden light tower was built on a square brick foundation about 16 feet high and 14 feet square. On the accompaning picture the light base is outlined by a dark rim. The strong fixed light was shaped like "Old Baldy's".

There was a keeper's dwelling located between the light and the present road. The back door of the house was about 100 feet from the tower down a little path. The typical plan was used for this dwelling except this one was a frame house. There was a full brick basement and the house is said to have been cool even in the heat of summer. It was "a story and a jump", with a porch across the front. There were two big rooms downstairs and two bedrooms upstairs. The separate kitchen was a large room with a Ship-Mate range.

The 1894 report of the Lighthouse Board, states that the storm of October 11-13, 1893, seriously injured the dwelling and the front beacon of the Oak Island Light Station. Due to changes in the channel at the entrance to the Cape Fear River rendering the lights at Oak Island useless to guide a vessel, the station was ordered discontinued on July 31, 1894.

During the hurricane men from the Life Saving Station had to evacuate the keeper, Captain George Walker, Mrs. Walker and their niece Susie Dosher, by boat. Buildings, including the keeper's house, were washed by high tides and blown by terrific winds across the bay to Southport, also dead cows, horses and chickens from the Light Station. Citizens still living in Southport tell of the terrible storm and of seeing parts of Captain Walker's house and stock washed ashore. Capt. Walker was perhaps the second and last keeper of this light station.

Mr. Rob Thompson, of Southport, born 1877, was Captain Walker's nephew. He liked to visit Uncle George and Aunt Sarah Ann (Dosher) when he was a boy of about twelve and they lived in the big house at the Light Station. They wanted to adopt him as they had no children of their own and he found this a very interesting family. His Aunt Sarah Ann was a sister of Esther Dosher ("Miss Ess") who had married Captain John Watts of the Life Saving Station, located then on Bald Head Island. His aunt's brother, Captain "Sonny" Dosher, kept Bald Head Lighthouse for thirty years. It is easy to imagine the lively conversations and experiences at Oak Island (Caswell) Light Station.

Mr. Rob talked of his boyhood visits there with eagerness, even as a man of eighty-nine years. His uncle let him help with the cleaning and care of the light. Together they climbed the tower steps to light the lamp that would help guide the ships to port. What more could a boy ask?

For quite a while the fuel for the light was kept in a small room behind the front stairs of the dwelling. Later a much safer arrangement was made; a small brick building was erected near the tower for storing the oil and supplies.

Mr. Rob remembers a Low Light at this station that was a mobile-type unit of strong timbers and could be moved as the channel changed so as to be of more assistance to the ships.

On an 1851 map of this area the sailing instructions read: "To enter Cape Fear River by Western Bar Channel when in 4 fathoms water bring the Bug Lights on Oak Island in range and keep that range N 35 ½' E passing either side of the buoy, until Bald Head Light bears E S E / S 67 ½ E and Cape Fear is open about 2 ships lengths to the Southward of the South Point of Bald Head Point when steer nearly parallel with the beach, until Bald Head Light bears S.E by E ¼ E.S 58° E. and the citadel in Fort Caswell E by E ¼ E' N 15 ½ E . . . . This channel must not be attempted without a pilot."

Because of the extreme dangers of entering the Cape Fear River, pilots were found to be necessary. Mr. Rob said his father, who was a pilot, was "as supple as a cat as he swung up anything he could get hold of to go aboard." The first pilot to board or speak to a vessel was given the job. of taking her to Wilmington and assumed complete charge of navigation once he was aboard. Keen competition developed, causing some of the men to move to Bald Head Island so as to be able to spot the incoming ships sooner than those who remained at Smithville (Southport). This is why Mr. Rob's family lived on Bald Head when he was just a boy.

The Pilot's Association was organized and has continued, though fewer pilots are required today because of modern navigation and communication. The old Pilot's Tower at City Dock was destroyed by a hurricane and was replaced by a modern metal tower near the old site.

About 1958 the top wooden tower on Oak Island was completely destroyed when men were burning brush nearby. They worked desperately to save the interesting old structure but the wood was dry and burned like a match box once the spark reached it. The brick foundation remains.

Many brave men have served in the Lighthouse Service of our country. Courageous men have built the towers, often at the risk of losing their lives. Countless stories of the heroism of lighthouse keepers have come down from generation to generation. Their faithfulness to duty has guided the ships past the dangers and safely into port. Here's to the men of the Lighthouse Service! Long may their kind continue.

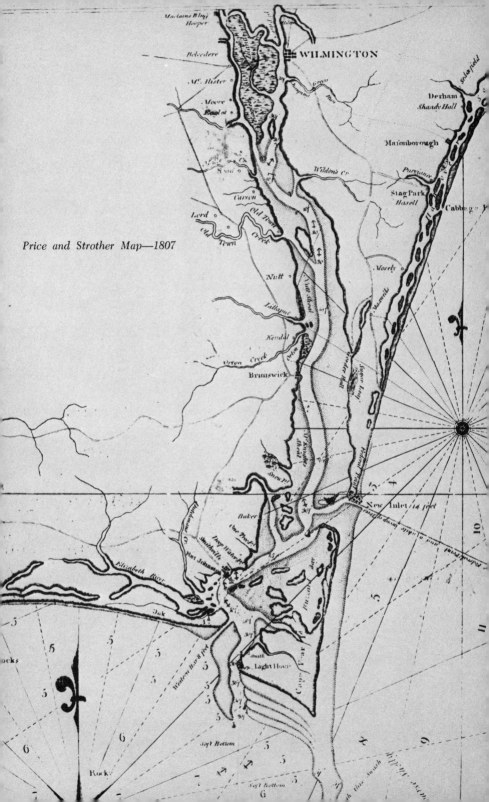

Price and Strother Map—1807

ACKNOWLEDGEMENTS

North Carolina Department of Archives and History
    Don Lennon, Richard W. Iobst, Mrs. Elizabeth Wilborn
United States Coast Guard
The Mariners Museum, John L. Lochheed—Librarian
Smith Island and the Cape Fear Peninsula—Cooper and Satterthwaite
State Port Pilot, Southport
The State, Bill Sharpe, editor
Compton's Encyclopedia (1946 edition)
Greensboro Daily News
The Star-News Newspapers, Wilmington
School of Forestry, Duke University
North Carolina Wildlife Resources Commission
North Carolina Travel Information Division
Mr. Hugh Morton

APPRECIATION

Data for this writing has been gathered over a period of years. Not all sources can be listed; however the following list is an attempt to recognize encouragement and assistance. Sincere appreciation is expressed to all who in anyway helped to set the lamps of our imagination burning again in the lighthouses of the Lower Cape Fear, and to those who made it possible to relive the ninety-one eventful years in the life of Cap'n Charlie Swan—Keeper of the Lights.

Mrs. Margaret Swan Hood, and her husband Murley, without whose untiring help *Cap'n Charlie* would never have been written

Members of the Swan family

Dr. Robert M. Helm—for many of the illustrations that help to tell the story

Mr. Rob Thompson, Southport

Mr. and Mrs. Davis Herring, Southport

Mr. Laurence Sprunt, Orton Plantation, Wilmington

Mr. W. C. Merritt, Winston-Salem

Dr. Louise Hall, Duke University

Mr. William G. Faulk Jr., Brunswick Town Historic Site

Mr. William M. Reaves, Brunswick Town Historic Site Guide

Mrs. Alice Taylor, Winnabow

Mr. and Mrs. James H. Harper, Southport

Mrs. Art Newton, Southport

Mrs. A. L. Lewis, Caswell Beach

Mr. and Mrs. George S. Daniels, Goldsboro

Mrs. Sue King, Southport

Mr. Fred Smith, Southport

Mr. Johnny Potter, Southport

Mr. R. V. Asbury, Wilmington

Mrs. R. M. Helm, Winston-Salem

Mrs. K. T. Raynor, Winston-Salem

Mrs. Larry James, Winston-Salem

Mrs. Warren Carr, Winston-Salem

Mr. O. F. Fowler, Winston-Salem

Mr. Jerry Gay, Winston-Salem

Mr. Sheafe Satterthwaite, Tenafly, New Jersey

Miss Minnie Spencer Kallam, Winston-Salem

Mrs. John Erickson, Southport

PHOTO CREDITS

State Department of Archives and History—pages 72-73, 104, 107
N. C. Wildlife Resources Commission—pages 24-25, 29, 38
N. C. Travel Information Division—pages 30, 90-91
N. C. News Bureau—page 97
Coastal Geodetic Survey—page 22
Official Photograph, U. S. Coast Guard—pages 6, 64, 95
National Archives—page 76
Star-News Newspapers, Wilmington—page 101
State Port Pilot—pages 42, 53, 92
Art Newton Studios, Southport, pages 40-41, 82-83, 86
C. F. Korstain, Duke University—pages 31, 55
Hugh Morton—page 44
Dr. Louise Hall, Duke University—page 77
Greensboro Daily News—page 81
Mrs. Margaret Harper—page 111
R. V. Asbury, Wilmington—108
Mr. and Mrs. George S. Daniels—page 108
International Oceanographic Foundation—page 18
Harper's Pictorial History of Great Rebellion—page 102